D0555031

The Passion of Tiger Woods

A JOHN HOPE FRANKLIN CENTER BOOK

The Passion of Tiger Woods

AN ANTHROPOLOGIST
REPORTS ON GOLF, RACE, AND
CELEBRITY SCANDAL

Orin Starn

DUKE UNIVERSITY PRESS
Durham & London 2011

© 2011 Duke University Press
All rights reserved
Printed in the United States of America on acid-free paper ♾
Designed by Jennifer Hill
Typeset in Scala by Tseng Information Systems, Inc.

Library of Congress Cataloging-in-Publication Data appear
on the last printed page of this book.

For Katya

Contents

Prologue

A very small boy, only two, marched onto the set of *The Mike Douglas Show* back in 1978. He wore short pants and was adorably cute with bright brown eyes and a little golf bag over his shoulder with three clubs in it. The boy's father accompanied him. This tall, good-looking black man sported a red turtleneck, gold chain, and an Afro in the Mod Squad style of the 1970s.

"Ladies and gentlemen, Earl and Tiger Woods!," announced Mike Douglas, the host of what was then America's most popular daytime talk show. His eclectic roster of A-list celebrities included the likes of John Lennon, John Wayne, Malcolm X, Frank Sinatra, and the yippie anarchist Jerry Rubin. The tall, affable host had his own fans. "The only white man who ever made me moist," according to Eddie Murphy's randy three-hundred-pound grandma character in *The Nutty Professor*.

Two Hollywood legends, Jimmy Stewart and Bob Hope, co-hosted the day the toddler Tiger appeared. It made for a funky crazy quilt of Americana: the two aging white movie stars looking a bit awkward in their sidekick roles, the tiny Southern California golf

prodigy with his black father and Thai mother. The studio audience laughed and applauded when the small boy gripped a club and smacked the ball straight into an indoor net. That Tiger was a little brown kid in what most Americans still thought of as a lily-white sport only added to the novelty.

Tiger Woods, at the age of two, on *The Mike Douglas Show* with (from left) Mike Douglas, Earl Woods, Bob Hope, and Jimmy Stewart, 1978.

Surely few viewers realized that they were witnessing a handover of the celebrity superstar baton. This toddler was not to be one of those child prodigies who flames out under unbearable expectations. Tiger would become perhaps the greatest golfer ever, and among the world's most famous faces. By his early thirties, he was a one-man multinational company, with enormous tournament winnings, corporate endorsements galore, the Tiger Woods EA Sports videogame franchise, and numerous other ventures. *Forbes* magazine heralded Woods as the first athlete to earn $1 billion. He and his blond-haired, blue-eyed wife, Elin Nordegren, seemed the poster couple for a shiny new postracial America with their two young children, two dogs, and the fabulous riches of Tiger's golfing empire.

All that changed in 2009. On the day after Thanksgiving, the news broke that Tiger had been in a car accident the night before. He'd crashed his black Cadillac Escalade into a fire hydrant just beyond the driveway of his and Elin's luxury home in a Florida gated community. Only few days before, a story in the *National Enquirer* had linked Tiger to a New York nightclub hostess. Now speculation began that Tiger and Elin had fought on Thanksgiving night, this somehow leading to his crash. In the following weeks, in fact, more than a dozen women came forward with tales of trysting with Tiger, among them a former reality-show contestant, a waitress, and a lingerie model. The scandal became headline news in *People, US,* and *Inside Edition,* as well as in supposedly more high-brow publications like the *New York Times,* not to mention fodder for countless jokes, blog posts, chat-room debates, and family conversations over holiday dinner. A Google search for "Tiger Woods scandal" quickly generated over one million hits.

That a famous golfer's sex life should have garnered more coverage than, say, the latest about global warming or the war in Afghanistan was a peculiar and perhaps disturbing sign of the times. Millions followed Tigergate's latest twists, but others were indeed disgusted that it received so much attention and attempted to ignore the whole affair. As an anthropologist, however, I had a special interest in Tiger's troubles. I teach a class about the anthropology of sports and, coincidentally, had been doing research about golf's strange, sometimes surprising role in modern American society. I'd long been fascinated by Tiger, owning the dubious distinction of having organized the first and only academic conference about the great golfer's role as a cultural icon and global brand. (Woods, perhaps justifiably enough, later snorted at a press conference about college professors not having anything "better to do" than sit around talking about him.) Although the ridicule may have been cosmic payback for his caddish behavior, I felt a bit sorry for Tiger, who had now become America's favorite target for opprobrious commentary and late-night talk-show jokes, and much more so for Elin and their children. But Tigergate also offered a whole new view of Tiger and the mythology that had surrounded him, and, more important, of the nature of sports, scandal, and racial and sexual politics in the country at large. It was a research mother lode for anyone interested in the bizarre funhouse and horror show of twenty-first-century American life.

This book is an anatomy of Tigergate. A star golfer's tabloid woes might seem an odd, if not frivolous, topic for an anthropologist. Anthropology, derived from the Greek words *anthropos* and *logos*, means simply the study of the human life, and in particular the vast diversity of cultures, traditions, and beliefs around the world. But in the era of disciplinary legends like Margaret Mead and Bronislaw Malinowski, anthropologists really only studied so-called primitive peoples in the jungles, deserts and islands of South Pacific, Africa, South America, and the planet's other far reaches. Those early researchers returned to write tomes with weighty titles like *The Mind of Primitive Man, Sex and Temperament in Three Primitive Societies*, and *Crime and Custom in Savage Society*. They left the study of modern industrial society to sociology under the curious early-twentieth-century academic division of labor. Even today, the stereotype of the anthropologist remains a pith-helmeted, Banana Republic-garbed recorder of exotic native customs in some distant Third World locale.

It's no longer accurate. Although we have new bugaboos, like a fondness for pretentious jargon, anthropologists today have expanded their range to study anybody, just about anywhere. You'll still find us with notebooks in hand in African villages and the misty Andean countryside (where I did research for many years earlier in my career), but also now in French biotech labs, San Francisco's S&M clubs, and the boardrooms of Japanese toy companies. Thus far, few of us have trained what the author and folklorist Zora Neale Hurston once called "the spyglass of anthropology" on sports, and yet more seem likely to do so as the discipline continues to broaden its scope. After all, whether it be the pregame singing of "The Star-Spangled Banner" at an American baseball game or the bacchanalian Brazilian celebration of a winning World Cup goal, sports abound in myth, ritual, and symbolism, those traditional topics of anthropological investigation. Now, too, we live in the era of what writer Kevin Quirk calls "SportsGlutUSA.' Continuous media coverage pipes the latest scores, signings, predictions, postmortems, and scandals into living rooms, bars, gyms, and airport waiting lounges nationwide, and increasingly around the world (and you could follow Tigergate on *Al-Jazzeera*, on the Paraguayan nightly news, and, of course, in the British tabloids). Sports have become too gigantic a part of global life for anyone to ignore, especially those of us who are supposed to be deciphering the workings of culture and society for a living.

As it happens, too, sports tell us more about ourselves and the world than one might expect. "Tell me what you play," as the French sociologist Roger Caillois once explained, "and I'll tell you who you are." Whether yoga, yachting, squash, boxing, or basketball, every sport draws most heavily from certain demographics, each with a sociology of its own. You don't find, for example, many impoverished teenage African American or Latino polo players (or, for that matter, white boxers from moneyed families). The larger tastes and temperament of a society may also sometimes be revealed in its games of choice. For example, Clifford Geertz, a well-known anthropologist, penned a classic essay that showed how a passion for cockfighting—and especially the intricate wagering around a match—mirrored the preoccupations with status, hierarchy, and bluffing and illusion in traditional Balinese culture. The modern American love affair with the NFL points to our own national obsessions with, well, gaudy spectacles, male bonding, brutal violence, and cheerleaders in skimpy outfits. Sports hold a mirror to society, no matter whether we like what we see there or not.

As much as it may also be yesterday's stale tabloid sleaze, the Tiger Woods scandal encapsulates a great deal about modern American realities. Most immediately, Tiger's tale takes us into the world of golf and the game's surprising place in our society. Golf has enough bizarre tribal customs to have delighted any old-time anthropologist, including those notorious plaid pants and an argot like "gimme," "flier," "scull," "fuab," "dogleg," "double break," and "chunk," which only another fairway initiate will understand. But it also occupies a much bigger part in American life than commonly assumed. Try taking the airplane test on your next flight: look out the window, and you'll notice courses everywhere down below. This nation has more than 17,000 golf courses, covering an area the size of Rhode Island and Delaware combined. They're as much a part of our strange modern ecology as the highway, the shopping mall, the reservoir, the strip mine, the missile silo, and the farm fields. More than twenty million Americans play golf; the golf industry employs another 400,000 between maintenance men, teaching professionals, driving-range operators, club industry executives, trade-magazine reporters, and many more. The first golf construction boom, just before the Great Depression, led the visiting Duke of Windsor to declare that America was "one vast golf course." It can seem truer than ever today.

I promise not to bore you with too much about golf in the following pages (and we'll soon get to the steamier topics of betrayal, raunchy sex, and race conflict). However, Tiger's case does afford an occasion for trying to figure out just why so many Americans play a game that many of their fellow citizens view as deadly dull or worse. That appeal has to do with the game itself and the special, sometimes addictive attraction it can exercise over those who take it up. (I must confess to being a golfer myself, though playing less often now after a string of back surgeries.) Golf has also long been the pastime of American business tycoons and politicians, all the way from Andrew Carnegie and William Howard Taft to Bill Gates, George W. Bush, and, yes, Barack Obama. A happy retirement to that gated Sunbelt golf community is the golden endpoint in a certain version of the American dream itself. At the same time, golf has always traced the fault lines of conflict, hierarchy, and tension in America, among them the archetypal divides of race and class. The fight to desegregate public golf courses and then professional golf, for example, is a fascinating, if little-known chapter in the Civil Rights movement. Nowadays, whether in Las Vegas or South Carolina's lowlands, you'll find five-star trophy courses for vacationing corporate moguls only a few miles from the run-down trailer parks where the Latino workers who do the course upkeep live. The geography of an America where the gap between the haves and have-nots has never been greater. There are low-cost, more plebeian traditions of golf in America, and yet the game will never be the sport of revolutionaries. It suits a Center-Right country where it's political suicide to talk too much about poverty, injustice, or taking away anyone's gas guzzlers or assault rifles.

The case of Tigergate also takes us beyond the manicured fairways into the world of sex and scandal. In its simplest form, this was a dismally prosaic domestic drama of marital infidelity, hardly a rarity in an America where more than half the marriages will end in divorce. But ours is a starstruck culture. We swoon over our sports, music, and movie celebrities, and yet also love to see them squirm, suffer, and feel our righteous rage when they misbehave. There was plenty of embarrassing, titillating, sometimes X-rated material for the gossip blogs and tabloids to report, between the likes of Tiger's raunchy "sexts" to a porn starlet and a panicky voicemail pleading for another lover to turn off her cell phone I.D. so Elin wouldn't get wind of their affair. And, of course, the mathematics of celebrity scandal means that the bigger the star, the bigger the scandal; Tiger was blessed and cursed to be among the biggest stars of all. That Woods had seemed such a straight arrow until that Thanksgiving night lent an extra element of drama and surprise to the plot line. It was no surprise that Tiger's troubles beat out such other momentous developments as Jessica Simpson's weight gain and a pair of reality-show hopefuls crashing a White House dinner to top About .com's list of the "ten hottest scandals" in 2010.

All this makes Tigergate good ground for plumbing the place of celebrity scandal in contemporary American culture. As much as we might prefer to ignore them, these tawdry dramas have become a multibillion-dollar business for a sector of the media, and their protocol is now every bit as ritualized as any village initiation ceremony. There's the breathless reporting of transgression; the blogosphere and tabloids digging for more evidence; the celebrity's attempt to evade, stonewall, or make excuses; and, of course, the solemn, sometimes teary public apology with an eye toward rehabilitation. We've seen it countless times, among politicians (Bill Clinton, Mark Sanford, Anthony Weiner), famous athletes (Michael Vick, Marion Jones), and, though we give them more license for misbehavior, movie stars and others entertainers (Mel Gibson, David Letterman). Tiger, a man who named his yacht *Privacy*, had always tightly controlled access to his private and family life. But even the proud, guarded Woods found himself swept along by the demands of scandal's cultural script, including at last the requisite apology before the cameras. His case very much followed the expected conventions of celebrity scandal, with its media frenzy, social psychology of public stoning, and the opportunity for the repentant sinning star later to be forgiven and reinstalled in the pantheon of the admired.

Most scandals may follow a similar script, yet each has its own special twists and turns (and they wouldn't be entertaining otherwise). One turn that Tigergate took was into the archetypal American trouble spot of race and race politics. Tiger's mixed heritage had made him a flashpoint for controversy early in his career, but the color of his skin seemed to matter less and less as he ascended the Olympus of golf legend and American glory. The revelations about Tiger's serial infidelity—and details like his seeming interest only in white women—reopened the matter of his racial identity in sometimes very ugly ways. Suddenly, for example, Tiger's penis size became the object of much interest and speculation in the tradition of white fear, anxiety, and voyeurism surrounding the supposedly greater bedroom prowess of black men. This and much else about Tigergate showed an America angry, afraid, transfixed, curious, and resentful about racial politics in both old and new ways.

None of these troubles had been in the Woods master plan. It was the quest for golfing excellence that had dominated Tiger's life almost from the cradle. His father, Earl, set up a highchair so his baby son could watch him hit golf balls into a practice net in the garage of their suburban Southern California home. When the tiny Tiger showed aptitude for the game, Earl, a former army colonel and Green Beret, dedicated himself to training the boy, intending to transform him into the world's best golfer in the tradition of the stage parent.[1] Tiger, who called Earl both his best coach and best friend, made his father's dream his own. He recorded a score of 48 for nine holes at the age of three, an incredible golfing feat for a toddler (and, in fact, Tiger appeared on the hit television show *That's Incredible!* not long after his Mike Douglas cameo). You can't understand much about Tiger and his story without knowing something about the game that was the foundation of his fame and identity.

And so let me begin with a bit more about golf and its peculiar place in our society.

1

GOLF BACKWARD SPELLS "FLOG"

G olf attracts among the most fanatical devotees of any sport. A group called the Golf Nut Society of America gives out an annual prize for "Golf Nut of the Year." One recent winner got the award for having collected more than 1,200 golf pencils; assembled a library of more than 2,520 golf books; and "struck all three of his sisters with golf shots." The former basketball superstar Michael Jordan won the prize for skipping the ceremony where he was to receive the NBA Most Valuable Player award in favor of thirty-six holes with friends. Every year, dozens of golfers ignore subzero temperatures, cracking icebergs, and roving polar bears to compete in Greenland's World Ice Golf Championships. Competitors use bright red and orange balls so as not to lose them in the snow.

Many other Americans detest golf as a boring, snotty game for rich white men with too much free time on their hands. "I'd rather," the comedian George Carlin once said, "watch flies fuck." The World Anti-Golf Movement, based in Japan, cites the game's supposedly harmful environmental and social consequences to advocate that courses everywhere be converted into public parks or restored to their natural state. It's a familiar component of Left-leaning, Whole Foods-shopping, Prius-driving white identity to dislike golf, or tolerate it as at best a useful, somewhat pathetic diversion for older relatives.

The negative stereotypes do not always hold up. Golf has a democratic tradition going back to its hardscrabble Scottish origins.[1] In America, ever since the golf boom of the early twentieth century, there have been plenty of affordable public courses for the golf-minded.[2] You'll find everyone from high-school kids and Walmart cashiers to retired plumbers at these plebeian tracks nowadays. Indeed, most American golfers come from the middle and working classes. Golf also has the oldest and among the most successful women's professional league of any sport. Babe Didrikson Zaharias, the legendary Olympic champion and protofeminist godmother to the Title IX generation, cofounded the Ladies Professional Golf Association back in the 1950s. Unlike, say, soccer or football, golf can be played by people of any age; and it's a myth that the game has to be expensive. Affluent golf nuts will spend thousands on the latest shiny high-tech clubs, but you can get a perfectly good used set for a hundred dollars on Craigslist. The game even has an admirable charitable-fundraising tradition, with dozens of benefit tournaments nationwide for causes from Teach for America to disabled war veterans. The men's professional tour raises more money for charity than any other major sport.[3] One young star, Ryo Ishikawa, donated his entire 2011 prize money to earthquake relief in his native Japan, more than a million dollars.

Golf lives down to its reputation in other respects. The archetypal blue-blooded East Coast country clubs were WASP-only. Some early

Mildred "Babe" Didrikson Zaharias, the Olympic legend who became a top golfer and co-founder of the women's professional tour, 1951. Photo by Julian P. Graham. Courtesy of Loon Hill Studios.

ideologues went so far as to claim that the game, as a pastime of "merry old England," was suitable only for those of "Saxon blood." Famous early American golf clubs, like Philadelphia's Merion Country Club, excluded blacks and Jews well into the twentieth century.[4] "We just don't do things that way in Birmingham," explained the

Black caddy and white golfer at the Pinehurst Resort, ca. 1935. African Americans, while barred from playing many courses, often labored as caddies and groundskeepers in the Jim Crow era. Some young blacks picked up the game from working at country clubs, including the pioneering pro Charles Sifford. Courtesy of Tufts Archives, Pinehurst, North Carolina.

club president at Alabama's Shoal Creek Country Club, with regard to barring blacks as late as 1990. Golf was also the last major professional sport to desegregate. It had a "Caucasians-only" clause until 1961, almost fifteen years after Jackie Robinson had broken baseball's color barrier. Two of America's most storied clubs — New Jersey's Pine Valley and Georgia's Augusta National—still do not allow female members. As for golf garb, there's no denying its unloveliness, straight down to the garish pants, white leather belts and the two-tone, fake leather cleats. "Golf," as another comedian, Robin Willams, quips, "is the only sport where a white man can dress like a black pimp."

But country club bigotry led excluded minority groups to build their own golf courses. Already by the 1920s, Jewish enthusiasts had founded the Century Club in White Plains, Chicago's Lakeshore Country Club, and other new establishments.[5] The black professional classes also banded together to start clubs, among them the legendary Langston Golf Club in 1939. This course was named for the black Civil War hero, pioneering lawyer, and Howard University trustee George Langston, who was also the uncle and namesake of the Harlem Renaissance author Langston Hughes. Black celebrity royalty like Cab Calloway, Billy Eckstine, and Joe Louis played at Langston often. A big oak on the fifth hole there became known as the "Joe Louis Tree" because the heavyweight champion hooked so many drives into it. (You can still play the course today, with its fairways bordered by the tough inner-city projects of Anacostia, Maryland, and the elevated subway clattering by.) In the age of Jim Crow, black baseball stars had been barred from the major leagues, heading instead to the Negro Leagues. The main professional golf tour, the PGA, also excluded blacks, and top black golfers turned to the United Golf Association, which was established with the financial backing of Joe Louis and others. This circuit played on substandard courses for small prizes, but nonetheless produced its own Satchel Paiges and Josh Gibsons, among them Teddy Rhodes, Bill Spiller and Eural Banks. Rhodes was so good that he'd later be dubbed the "black Jack Nicklaus."

Several black players, in fact, excelled on the men's professional tour once it dropped its "Caucasians-only" clause. The cigar-chomping Charlie Sifford, the first man to break golf's color line,

Joe Louis (far right) with (from left to right) the early black golf legends Leonard Reed (who was also a well-known singer), Bill Spiller, and Teddy Rhodes. Courtesy the American Golfer.

won three tournaments, despite being well past his prime by the time he was allowed his playing card (and, to anyone who asked, cited Norman Vincent Peale's *The Power of Positive Thinking* as his favorite book). Other men of color from humble backgrounds also made their marks. Rod Curl, a Native American from a small Cali-

Lee Trevino, the great Latino golf pioneer, with friend and rival Jack Nicklaus, 1971. Courtesy of AP Wide World Photos.

fornia Indian tribe almost exterminated in the Gold Rush, stood down the blond über-golfer Nicklaus to win the prestigious Colonial National Invitational one year. The short, skinny Juan "Chi Chi" Rodriguez was a Puerto Rican street urchin who got into golf caddying at an island country club. Rodriguez defied the laws of physics by blasting some of the game's longest drives and was known for his trademark Zorro-like faux rapier thrusts of the putter whenever he holed a long one.

My favorite old-time golfer is Lee Trevino. Trevino grew up poor in a dirt-floored shack outside Dallas, with his washerwoman mother and gravedigger grandfather. He picked up golf while driving a tractor at a local practice range and was soon hustling locals by betting he could beat them playing with only a Dr. Pepper bottle wrapped in masking tape for a club. Even after becoming one of the world's best players, Trevino faced the syrupy condescension that is hatred's flip side of the American racial coin. According to one journalist, he was "a constantly chattering, joking little Mexican;" *Golf Digest* likewise noted the "carefree Mexican heritage" of this "gay young caballero."[6] The tricksterish Trevino himself was not always averse to the old happy-go-lucky, Frito Bandito, Taco Bell, noontime-siesta image of Mexico and Mexicans. He billed himself the "Merry Mex" and once joked he'd buy back the Alamo for Mexico after winning the 1971 U.S. Open (only later to announce that he'd changed his mind on discovering that the old fort had no indoor plumbing). But Trevino's humor could also be biting about his hard childhood and the realities of American society. "I was twenty-one years old," he liked to say, "before I realized that Manual Labor wasn't a Mexican."

Golf has remained very much associated with the establishment, despite the Curls and the Trevinos. From its first years in America, after the Civil War, the game was the preferred sport of leading industrialists, the culture heroes of American business. Andrew Carnegie, that archetypal robber baron and philanthropist, loved golf from his Scottish childhood; Bill Gates got married on the twelfth tee of Hawaii's Manele Bay Golf Club, and was part-owner of a course; Warren Buffet, America's other richest man, also follows in the tradition of the golfing tycoon (and, for that matter, so do hip-hop moguls like Jay-Z and Kanye West). Then and now, joining a fancy golf club is a way to set yourself apart from society's lower echelons, a hoi polloi-free zone, where you can enjoy prosperity's rewards in a gated, bucolic exclusivity.

The game also suits the spirit of capitalism. If business enshrines the individual and the glories of competition and the free market, then so does golf. You're on your own, no team sport this. That avid champion of capitalism, Rush Limbaugh, a lousy yet avid player himself, calls professional golfers the ultimate free-market entrepreneurs. Everything comes down to the individual's performance in this brand of survival of the fittest, the game being about the bottom line of the scorecard and its dicey mathematics of risks and rewards. More pragmatically, golf's pace is perfect for strengthening business relationships. A swing takes only about four seconds. This means that the average golfer spends just seven minutes or so of a typical four-hour round actually playing the game. That leaves plenty of time for socializing with your foursome and for networking that you can turn to your advantage. Also, many businessmen are of a certain age, and golf allows you to play almost to the grave (the singer and movie star Bing Crosby, for example, died of heart failure at seventy-four walking off the eighteenth hole at a Spanish course).

Golf has also long been the pastime of politicians. In the early twentieth century, it was still regarded as too much the rich man's sport for a political hopeful to enjoy, at least in public. "Horseback riding, yes," the ever manly Theodore Roosevelt advised his protégé William Howard Taft, "tennis, no. And golf is fatal."[7] But as the middle classes took to golf, it was no longer viewed as a liability to a president's image, when enjoyed in moderation. The rotund Taft ignored Roosevelt's advice and was often photographed on the course with club in hand. Almost every president since then (the only recent exception being the NASCAR-loving Jimmy Carter) has golfed. The best player among them was John F. Kennedy, in spite of his chronic back pain. Although a hacker Dwight Eisenhower was the biggest golf nut (and with his unassuming, grandfatherly profile did much to popularize the sport among America's expanding middle classes following the Second World War); the thirty-fourth president left spike marks across the Oval Office on his frequent way to practice chipping on the South Lawn. "Ben Hogan for President," read a bumper sticker in 1956: "If we're going to elect a golfer as president, let's have a good one." Barack Obama, who's not much better than Eisenhower, plays whenever he can get away for a few hours at military base courses around the Washington, D.C. area.

Golf would become associated with the very ideal of American power, prosperity, and luxury. "How many golf courses does Russia have?," crowed the famed golf-course architect Alister Macken-

Barack Obama at the golf course with an aide, 2009. Courtesy of AP Wide World Photos.

zie in 1930.[8] According to a certain Cold War way of thinking, the Communist Soviet Union was a dreary limbo of cheap vodka, bad borscht, and gray Stalinist high-rises, while Americans cavorted in a shiny Technicolor wonderland of lush green courses, cute electric golf carts, cheery pastel polo shirts and bermuda shorts, and tropical cocktails with little paper umbrellas at the nineteenth hole. When the United States won the race to the moon, in 1969, the Apollo astronauts read a passage from Genesis just before landing and, of course, planted the Stars and Stripes in the lunar desert; on the third moon mission, the astronaut Buzz Aldrin brought a golf club and, as millions watched on television, took a one-armed, zero-gravity, slow-motion pass at a golf ball. The United States, or so the some-what incongruous symbolism of the bible reading and that famous six-iron shot suggested, is a God-fearing, golf-playing nation. The affable Aldrin joked later that his shot sailed for "miles and miles" into the void; if this is true and not just a golfer's boast, some rough math indicates the little 5.2752 inch circumference sphere should now be halfway between Jupiter and Pluto. Golf was the first and, to this point, only sport played on the moon in the known history of the universe.

America's Cold War opponents had no affection for golf. In 1961 Fidel Castro, Cuba's new master, played an experimental round with his fellow revolutionary Ernesto "Che" Guevara (for which the two young, bearded comandantes both wore combat boots and their trademark guerrilla fatigues). Later, unimpressed by this pastime that stank to him of Yankee imperialism and big money, Castro ordered most of Cuba's courses plowed under. That other Marxist icon, Mao, also kept China a golf-free zone.

But golf was on the Cold War's winning side, and the post–1989 global ascendancy of American-style corporate culture, resort tourism, and the market economy has helped to spur a worldwide golf boom in the last few decades.[9] The modern geography of sports, it should be noted, often points toward older histories of power, empire, and cultural capital. The British, for example, exported cricket to their far-flung colonies; the game remains a staple in India, Pakistan, Australia, and other former crown possessions even today. Outside Spain, you'll find bullfighting only in one-time Spanish holdings like Peru and Mexico where the conquistadores brought their gory pastime. And so, as America triumphed in the Cold War, the archetypal capitalist game has gained a growing foothold in Russia and elsewhere in the former Soviet Union with dozens of courses springing up in recent years. Golf had already been popular in parts of East Asia, and yet interest is now far more widespread there than ever before. More than twenty million devotees play in Taiwan, Japan, and South Korea alone (and an astonishing forty of the top 100 female golfers in the world come from South Korea, for reasons that no one has yet adequately explained).[10] Sweden has be-

The revolutionary icon Ernesto "Che" Guevara, who learned golf in his Argentine youth, during an impromptu match with Fidel Castro, Havana, 1961. Photo by Alberto Korda.

come the world's most golf-addicted nation, with golfers numbering roughly 10 percent of the country's ten million people. And though the Great Helmsman's embalmed body may be shuddering in disgust, rising global China has built more than two hundred courses, including its own gated golf "communities" for the new rich. "Green opium," some have dubbed the game's addictive power there. Golf tourism to tropical-resort enclaves like Malawi, Dubai, and the Canary Islands has become a multibillion dollar business, sometimes displacing poor villagers.[11] The Castro brothers have even relented, now allowing luxury golf-resort construction to attract foreign vacationers to their cash-starved island. This is a golfing planet in the new millennium, the worst nightmare of those who detest the game.

Strangely, however, many golfers are not too sure they like golf so much themselves. On the face of it, the game would seem to be easy enough to master and then enjoy. Unlike in soccer or basketball, the ball is stationary, you hit only when you are ready, and you are not reliant on your teammates. The reality is that golf technique is hard to acquire quickly; it's not like, say, bowling, where you can get lucky and roll a strike the first time. Novice golfers often find themselves whiffing the ball altogether, and more practice by no means makes perfect. "Golf is a game," Winston Churchill complained, "whose aim is to hit a very small ball into an even smaller hole, with weapons singularly ill designed for the purpose." The perfectionist Ben Hogan, one of history's best players, calculated he hit only seven shots a round on the sweet spot. But the fact that the swing is always under your own control—and with no one but yourself to blame for that shank into the water hazard—makes the inevitable bad shots disheartening just the same, and many all the more so. Golfers frequently work themselves into thick lathers of despair, disgust, and self-loathing by a poor round's end. "Nice shot, asshole!," one of my playing partners will mutter to himself after snap-hooking a drive into the trees or some other miscue. The satirist P. G. Wodehouse noted that the game spells "flog" backward (both he and another early-twentieth-century literary notable, A. A. Milne, of *Winnie the Pooh* fame, were nonetheless frequent players).

Why, then, does anyone bother with golf? It has long been a matter of speculation among golfers, scholars, and others as to just why so many people play despite the abundant frustrations. A couple of decades ago, when it seemed that the discovery of DNA and the magic of evolutionary theory could explain everything about human behavior, the Harvard biologist Edward O. Wilson conjured the hypothesis that humans have a "golf gene" going back millions of years: flying projectiles supposedly enchant us because hunting meant survival for those protohuman Australopithecines on Africa's plains. According to this theory, natural selection has left us with a gene pool disposed to grasslands and panoramic views good for hunting, as compared to the more forested topography that early humans supposedly left behind in transitioning to savannah life. In stepping onto the course, claims one of Wilson's supporters, we may be "reenacting the steps taken by some hominid a hundred thousand generations in the past, steps that helped him or her become our ancestors." And what's more: "It could even be that the clubs we carry remind us, on some instinctive level, of the tools they carried in search of food."[12]

I can't say I'm altogether convinced. It's surely a very long way from Australopithecus Africanus, stone tools, and dead wildebeests to the chunky vacationer in bermuda shorts flailing at a little white sphere with an oversized titanium driver. The modern golfer forages in the grill room. And a preference prevails there for fatty, decidedly maladaptive foods like hot dogs, potato chips, and mayonnaise-drenched chicken salad. If humans have a "golf gene," it must be recessive since so many people think the game is a waste of time or worse. Unless, Walter Hagen forbid, some wacky geneticist decides to make it his next research project, this particular Darwinian golfing thesis will stay in the drawer of unproven scientific theories along with Bigfoot, UFO sightings, and the Loch Ness monster.

As a dutiful anthropologist, I've interviewed dozens of golfers, trying to figure out the spell cast by golf. The game's most elementary lure, or so many report, is that flush of satisfaction and even inner delight that comes from hitting a good shot: a twisting twenty-five-foot putt curving into the hole; a clever escape from under the trees; a drive launched long and true into the big blue sky. None of us will ever know the ecstasy of running as fast as Usain Bolt or cutting through the water like Michael Phelps. But at least once every time out, even a rotten golfer will hit a shot as magnificent as if it had been struck by Tiger Woods himself. It's an addictive small brush with the sublime. Golfers speak about that one shot in a round that "keeps you coming back" or, as if that perfect moment were a fuzzy teddy bear or a tab of Ambien, the "shot to go to sleep with."

That satisfaction recalls one of Sigmund Freud's famous cases.[13] Freud described a toddler who was so attached to his mother that he'd cry when she left the room. The boy invented a game where he'd tie a length of string to a wooden spool and then throw it into his curtained crib, exclaiming, "Gone." Then he'd pull it back out with a happy "There!" As Freud might also have said about golf (his own favorite diversion being a three-handed Slovenian card game called tarok), the endless playing of this crude game was a form of "repetition compulsion." But it provided the boy what Freud called a "pleasurable illusion of power," a feeling of control that contrasted with his actual helplessness about his mother's movements. According to a more recent psychology experiment, this same pleasure at the momentary mastery of an inscrutable universe appears to be at work for blind babies, who smile when they learn to make a bell jingle by tapping it with their foot.

Golfers resemble those blind babies. In the instant of that rare good swing, where the ball rises off the club face toward the pin on just the intended aim and trajectory, they seem to feel the small gratification of having done something right, with the realities of death, taxes, and life's cruelty suspended in those evanescent seconds. That so many of our shots go awry make these occasional successes all the sweeter, and even more so those very rare periods when we get into that mystical "zone" of playing for a stretch beyond our usual abilities.[14]

There's also a peculiar metaphysics of hope and optimism at work, the proverbial string-end carrot. As dreadfully as you may have performed for the first few holes, you always have the chance of redemption on the next shot, the back nine, or, if things have gotten too bad that day, the next round. The culture of early-twenty-first-century America trumpets the possibilities of self-improvement through the quick fix: the crash diet to lose a few pounds; the cram course to raise your SAT scores; the Botox to smooth those wrinkles. As the wry golf writer Herbert Warren Wind already noted in 1954, the golfer also often believes that "he is on the verge of 'coming into his own' and that if he corrects one tiny movement—the way he bends his left knee or the position of his right thumb—then his swing will become a vision of beauty and even-par scores will be no trouble at all."[15] You'll find every manner of sometimes bizarre instruction in golf magazines, books, and instructional videos. (Imagine you are trying to hit the ball through a ring of fire! Practice putting with a broom to learn that sweeping motion! Place a tennis shoe behind your club to slow down the takeaway on your backswing!) That golfers always think they *could* improve under the right training regimen introduces a pleasing element of possibility (and every forty-something club golfer of some ability seems to believe that he could play on the senior professional tour if only he dedicated himself full-time to the game).

Golf is also a last chance to do that most childish of things, play, and in this sense it's no surprise that so many older people like the game. To head to the course is to return to the sandbox, the pleasures of the playground. Exact repetition bores adults, in contrast to the toddler's delight at playing peekaboo over and over again. But the variation of each shot and golf course—as trivial an index of variety as it might seem to the outsider—allows for the sensation of "novelty" that Freud called "the precondition of enjoyment" for grown-ups. We may be destined to hit many more bad shots than good. But the swing, like the levers on that yellow sandbox dump truck, remains ours to control in the make-believe world of the golf course. Fantasy is essential to play, and golfers love to dream about making a hole-in-one, a personal best score, or winning the club championship. I always feel a twinge of pleased anticipation before teeing off, no matter that fantasy almost always runs afoul of reality before I am too far into the round.

Toys are part of play, and few games can match golf's staggering selection of equipment choices between clubs, balls, gloves, shoes, head covers, bags, apparel, telescoping contraptions for retrieving golf balls from water hazards, and training gadgets of every kind. A trip to a big box store like Golf Galaxy and Pro Golf Discount is the grown-up golfer's equivalent of a childhood expedition to Toys-R-Us, with the same tempting rows of shiny goods, intriguing shapes and colors, and new product smell. As a matter of having the right "tools," golf gear tends to be a male obsession, with more than its fair share of phallic symbolism. Equipment companies cater shamelessly to our desires for greater size and length. "L" (for long), "B" (for big), "D" (for distance), "X" (for large), and "XL" (for extra large) have long been preferred letters in the lexicon for ball names; manufacturers like to string them together with a few other meaningless numbers or symbols for that extra aura of high-tech engineering (the Titleist ProVI-X, Top-Flite XL/Distance, Bridgestone B330-RXS, and so on). The United States Golf Association sets limiting distance standards for balls and clubs, but every company nonetheless seems to claim that its "new and improved" latest product is the "longest ball" and the "longest driver." They promise "greater length," "huge distance," and "improved performance," with plenty of faux-scientific graphs and charts to back up the claims of increased potency. Golf equipment is Viagra for middle-aged men who've lost a bit over the years or for younger ones who just want to be the biggest studs in their foursomes. (Female golfers, also true to these lowest-common-denominator gender stereotypes, spend more of their money on golf apparel than on equipment.)

The oversized metal drivers of the last two decades have actually made a big difference for the average golfer. It was hard to hit with the smaller, wooden clubs of my youth; the modern titanium-alloy drivers are vastly more forgiving, and the ball travels much farther. But you have to be a very good golfer to benefit much from other technology advances—the latest aerodynamic golf ball won't help if you don't get the ball off the ground in the first place; the newest irons don't work that much better than those of a few decades ago, despite the advertising hype and price tags upward of $3,000 a set; and an ultra-high-tech $500 magnesium-alloy putter won't save you from the shakes on the greens (and, in fact, the best putter among my golfing friends uses a beat-up 1983, Bullseye-brand Acushnet model). Wanting to have the latest equipment has much more to do with golf's psychology of possibility, hope, and the fresh start than anything else. It's one of the game's small pleasures to try out that new club, no matter that it will more often than not end up disappointing in the end, maybe even winding up broken over a knee or flung into a lake, as golfers will do when they get very angry with their poor play.

That luck figures into the equation is an additional part of golf's appeal for those who enjoy the game. Golf is a game not just of skill, but also of chance: the way the ball happens to hit a tree or just miss it, to roll into a water hazard or stop inches short of it. In the long run, of course, it all evens out, though golfers tend nonetheless to obnoxious griping about the bad bounce and to forget all the times a lucky carom went their way. But as dispiriting as the bad break can be, the pleasure of those moments when Tyche, the Greek goddess of luck, smiles your way is part of golf's lure, like finding yourself with a winning ticket at the horse races. Will that putt hang on the edge of the hole—or topple in after a tantalizing few moments, as did, for example, Tiger Woods's amazing chip shot on the sixteenth hole of the 2005 Masters? Golf can be a spin of the roulette wheel, with the same tense anticipation and, when the ball does rattle into the cup as if into the winning number, that same feeling of everything being right with the world. The biggest jackpot is the hole-in-one. Although the pros make so many that they merit little more than smiling high fives with their caddies, it's a big deal for any other golfer to mark down a "1," or an "ace" in golfing parlance. The chance of the average player doing so—and it's only on short holes, par threes, that it's typically even possible—are approximately 80,000 to 1. At country clubs in an older day, they sold hole-in-one insurance, to pay for the free drinks you were expected to buy for every member if you made one. Many local charity tournaments now designate a hole where you'll win a free car or even a million dollars for a hole-in-one (and tournament organizers buy special insurance against the unlikely event of it happening).

That golf gets you outdoors forms another dimension of its attraction. It's no coincidence that this Scottish pastime took root in America in the late nineteenth century and early twentieth (the very first club was established only in 1885, in the bucolic Hudson River Valley). If you've plowed fields all day under a hot sun, spending still more time outdoors is not likely to top your wishlist of ways to relax. And yet, as so many more Americans found themselves cooped in factories and offices in an industrializing nation, the idea of getting out into nature became newly attractive. The century's turn saw the birth of the Sierra Club and the Audubon Society; the first national parks; a boom in gardening; the naturalistic Arts and Crafts architecture movement, with its exposed wood and stone; and the new popularity of activities like hiking, archery, and mountain climbing. A belief that too much civilization and the hustle and bustle of city living isn't healthy for anyone remains very much a part of the American zeitgeist.

Many people, of course, see golf as a sorry excuse for a more genuine outdoor experience. It is often asserted that golf courses actually harm the environment. The game conjures images of bull-dozed wilderness, wasted water, and the tons of pesticides, fertilizer, and herbicides required to generate that velvety green carpet look. Clearly, nitrogen fertilizer runoff sometimes damages local watersheds, and the amount of water demanded for course maintenance can be large indeed (desert clubs in Arizona, Nevada, and Southern California alone suck millions of scarce gallons a year). A golf course is always, in fact, simultaneously a living organic thing and an artificial human invention, an example of what the French theorist Bruno Latour calls "nature-culture."[16] But few courses are built on pristine forest any longer, and many occupy recycled land like abandoned quarries and landfills. By comparison to the asphalted shopping centers and parking lots that might otherwise be built on the same land, golf courses generate oxygen and cool the atmosphere, a benefit in the age of global warming. They very often also become refuges for wildlife with no place else to go (the best place to spot turtles, foxes, deer, or even bears, mountain lions, and crocodiles is very often your nearest course). New environmentally minded courses—the golf fanatic and pop star Justin Timberlake has built a model in Memphis—recycle waste water for irrigation; they also incorporate wetlands and unkempt natural areas into their designs to minimize chemical fertilizing and mowing. No study has yet tried to calculate the overall carbon footprint of America's endless acres of golf courses (and any such calculation should include all the gas golfers burn up annually driving out to play). It seems fair to say that golf courses, while having their harmful consequences, do not rank among our most pressing environmental worries.

I do think that golf speaks to a certain American ambivalence about the idea of nature itself. As much as we may love our World Wildlife Foundation calendar, few of us actually want to rough it in the wilderness without plenty of fancy backpacking gear, or make the perilous, oxygen-deprived attempt to scale a lonely mountain peak. We tend to what might be called the "RV syndrome," namely the wish to escape city living without leaving the Mr. Coffee machine, the French onion dip, and the rest of civilization's creature comforts too far behind. Golf matches these unadventurous ambitions perfectly. You get to spend half a day out in some facsimile of the great heart of nature, but without the dirt and the danger, never too far from the snack shack and a cold beer. That each course is as different in its way as the land itself contributes to the sensation of a domesticated sort of outdoors experience. Some golfers keep a souvenir ball imprinted with the logo of each new track they've played, just like Boy Scouts collect patches for every park they've visited.

Many golfers have their own idiosyncratic reasons for liking the game. The loner finds a hermit's solace in a pastime that allows you to be alone in the thin twilight of a winter day (those who like to socialize have the ritual weekend foursome); the basement do-it-yourselfer can tinker with his clubs or even make his own; and the gambler has the Nassau, Bingo Bango Bongos, sandies, and other such abstruse bets and side bets with his foursome. What Herbert Warren Wind termed golf's "wondrous flexibility" may not convince a majority of Americans of its worth ("a tragic waste of real estate," sighs one friend of mine). The game, however, does have something for a variety of different personality types.

These charms are not enough to keep some golfers in the fold. How many old sets of clubs languish unused in America's carports? Thousands quit golf every year for lack of time and money, or due to frustration. Some pick it up again; others don't. Golf, a luxury, takes a special hit in periods of economic hardship. Almost no new courses were built during the Great Depression, and some three hundred closed in the more recent recession of 2008. Some of those who keep at it do so against their better instincts. Carl Adatto, a psychiatrist who wrote about the psychology of golf, once described a patient who went out every day even though he always hated it. "Thank God it's raining today," the man would think to himself, "so I don't have to play."[17]

2

THE TIGER WOODS REVOLUTION

The world of golf found a charismatic young ruler in Tiger Woods. Tiger left Stanford University in 1996 to turn pro with a $40 million dollar endorsement contract from Nike. Phil Knight, the billionaire Nike founder had followed the skinny college student at an Oregon tournament and decided to sign him no matter the cost. Tiger's breakout victory came a year later at Augusta National's Masters Championship, when he was twenty-one. Woods won by eleven shots, recording the lowest score ever at this celebrated tournament. Shell-shocked veteran pros wondered at the new superstar's titanic drives, jeweler's touch around the greens, and uncanny, almost ferocious will and concentration. "He plays a game with which I'm not familiar," said Jack Nicklaus, whom most experts had agreed was history's finest player until Tiger began challenging his records.[1]

Other observers saw an America turned upside down. "It's crazy, man," said the basketball star turned television commentator Charles Barkley, "the best golfer in the world is black, and the best rapper is white" (the rape- and incest-themed gothic stylings of Marshall Mathers, Eminem, then topped the charts). Tiger was the first African American to win one of golf's coveted four major championships: the Masters, the U.S. Open, the British Open (or "The Open Championship" as the organizers of this, the oldest major, more grandly prefer it), and the PGA.[2] His Masters triumph had special significance. The only blacks allowed at the hosting Augusta National Golf Club in the Jim Crow–era had been the maids, waiters, caddies, and shoeshine "boys." Club officials did not invite one of "our dark-complected friends," as the club co-founder Clifford Roberts once put it, to compete in the Masters until 1975.[3]

Tiger received a hero's acclaim for his triumph. President Bill Clinton, another golf nut, phoned congratulations. Every magazine, newspaper, and news show in America covered the dramatic victory of the handsome young champion and his famous, teary, eighteenth-hole hug with father Earl, which had capped his triumphant round. In a bit of fatherly hyperbole, Earl predicted that his son would be much more than a great golfer. "Tiger will do more than any other man in history to change the course of humanity," the elder Woods predicted, "be bigger than Gandhi and Buddha. . . . He is the Chosen One."[4] A starstruck fan, only half-jokingly, set up a website called the First Church of Tiger Woods. It was dedicated "to examining the possibility that God is walking the earth as a 21st century, multi-ethnic, superstar golfer and whether that is any more or less likely than God coming in the form of a first-century, Jewish carpenter."[5]

It soon became apparent that Tiger was actually not very interested in spirituality or any sort of outspoken social activism. He followed the pathway of his good friend and predecessor as America's best-known athlete, Michael Jordan, who studiously avoided controversy so as to focus on his sport and to maximize his commercial potential as a pitchman for Nike and other companies. Jordan was once asked why he didn't endorse a candidate seeking to unseat a race-baiting Republican senator in his home state of North Carolina. "Republicans," the basketball god had replied. "wear tennis shoes, too." Sports scholars Peter Kaufman and Eli Wolf argue that society has generally discouraged athletes from becoming social activists.[6] The U.S. Olympic Committee sending home sprinters John Carlos and Tommie Smith for their black-power medal stand salute at the 1968 Olympics is one famous example.[7] Most young sports stars nowadays live in a cocoon of training, competition, and celebrity. They do not necessarily know or care enough about the wider world to want to take a stand on controversial matters of politics and social justice. A general expectation does now exist that prominent sports figures should "give back" through some charity work, but most stick to "safe" causes like fighting cancer or helping children. In this vein, Woods established the Tiger Woods Foundation to raise money for educational enrichment, especially for underprivileged children. His father, Earl, was the first director and the foundation held an annual Las Vegas concert fundraiser with stars like Keith Urban, John Mayer, and M.C. Hammer. Tiger Jam raised millions for the Tiger Woods Foundation and selected area charities.

But Woods seemed to spend most of his energy away from the course cashing in on his fame. He filmed dozens of commercials and made countless appearances for a portfolio of sponsors that included Buick cars, TAG Heuer watches, Gillette razors, Gatorade, and American Express. Nike did not have a golf line before Tiger, but they built a multibillion dollar business in apparel, balls, and clubs on the strength of his endorsement. Woods was featured in the ubiquitous airport billboards for Accenture, the giant consulting company. That campaign targeted the corporate road warriors who very often play golf. "Go On," the billboards enjoined, "Be a Tiger." By 2009, Tiger's career endorsement earnings alone exceeded $300 million. Woods explained to *Sports Illustrated* that his goal was to "ensure the financial security of my family," as if the nearly one billion dollars he had already made between his endorsements and tournament winnings were not enough. He and Elin paid more than $40 million for a twelve-acre lot on Florida's ultra-exclusive Jupiter Island, with plans to build a new mansion there.[8]

Tiger also transformed professional golf. Viewers with only marginal interest in the game tuned in to watch his latest fairway exploits. The high Nielsen ratings led to bigger television contracts for the professional tour and, in turn, ever-increasing purses. In a measure of our skewed winner-take-all society, where a CEO or a sports superstar routinely earns more than a hundred times more than a nurse or schoolteacher, the salaries of top athletes in every major sport have grown exponentially in the last few decades. But the rewards for golfers were among the fastest rising of any major sport thanks to Woods. When Tiger joined the tour, in 1996, the total annual prize money was less than $70 million; it had quadrupled to more than $280 million a decade later. Veteran pros might seldom beat Tiger, and yet they were still earning more than ever before. Woods was golf's golden goose. His fellow tour players, their caddies, and just about anyone else connected with the professional game gathered the financial rewards.

Tiger raised golf's profile everywhere. You couldn't avoid seeing him on television or on airport billboards everywhere across the planet. Woods became a global superstar, with millions of fans across the Americas, Europe, Oceania, and parts of Africa. Kultida Punsawad, a Bangkok native and an army secretary, had met and married Colonel Earl Woods in Thailand during the Vietnam War years. Thai society had tended to discourage local women from liaisons with black American soldiers; the offspring of such unions were sometimes described as having *phiu swai*, or "ugly skin."[9] But when Tiger arrived with Kultida, in 1997, to visit Thailand and play a tournament there, the Thais were so eager to claim Woods as one of their own that the foreign-affairs minister presented him with honorary citizenship and a royal medal. Kultida herself was half-Thai, half-Chinese. That Woods had an Asian mother made him all the more popular through the whole region.

Perhaps inevitably, Tiger's spectacular success tapped into the modern mythology about black athletic superiority.[10] As late as the mid-twentieth century, many ideologues of white supremacy held people of African descent to be inferior physically as well as mentally. "The negro," claimed one biologist in 1929, manifested "specific biological disabilities," "weakness," and "race deterioration" that made him into an "inferior organism."[11] Pioneering black athletes like Joe Louis and the Olympic champion Jesse Owens shattered these assumptions with their great achievements. By the late twentieth century, the conventional wisdom had flipped, the new paradigm holding blacks to be better athletes than whites, and including the supposition, as the hit Hollywood movie had it, that "white men can't jump." It's true enough that sprinters of West African descent have posted the top two-hundred times ever recorded in the 100 meter dash; East Africans thoroughly dominate distance running; or, for that matter, Eurasian whites normally sweep the Olympic medals in the strength events. Genetic variation across human populations likely does play some role in sports success, albeit not along the crudely drawn lines of black and white in any simple way.[12] But athletic excellence is always far more than a simple matter of biology. The making of sports stars depends on the complex, poorly understood interaction of factors like heredity, nutrition and training, good coaching, and the cultural premium a society places upon a given sport. Consider, after all, that two relatively small European countries, Italy and Spain, hoisted the last two

World Cup trophies, reigning supreme at the planet's most popular pastime. It's ultimately that rare, color-blind alchemy of dedication to training, performance under pressure, and a passionate will to win that sets a Michael Phelps, a Michael Jordan, or a Lionel Messi apart from the rest. Creepily, too, the myth of black athletic superiority, whatever may be its at most very limited basis in fact, often pairs up with the hateful stereotype of inferior black intellectual ability, and the demeaning caricature of the strong yet dumb n—, which dates back to slavery.[13] Thus, for example, the Los Angeles Dodgers vice-president Al Campanis could, in 1987, explain that the dearth of African American baseball managers was due to blacks lacking the mental "necessities," as opposed to patterns of discrimination and the white old-boy network that has and sometimes still does dominate hiring in that sport.

As for golf, some observers had developed the folk theory that blacks were physiologically ill-suited to the game. When queried about the paucity of African American pros in 1994, the golf great Jack Nicklaus suggested that "blacks have different muscles that react in different ways."[14] If people of West African descent abounded in the so-called fast-twitch muscle fibers for speed and power, then they lacked the "slow-twitch" ones supposedly needed for golf, or so this crude and altogether unsubstantiated hypothesis about race, anatomy, and golf excellence had it. But Tiger's prodigious success put an end to the theory of black golf inferiority. Now, in fact, the whispering winds of racial speculation and stereotyping started to blow in the opposite direction. It began to be hinted and sometimes asserted that, far from a handicap, being black gave Tiger an "innate" advantage. Although it's less common today, sports announcers in the 1990s often tended to describe black athletes as having "natural" talent and athleticism, and the white ones as "hardworking," "scrappy," and "intelligent." All the talk about the young Tiger's "superior" power, quickness, and explosiveness followed in this larger coverage pattern, and its patronizing implications that African American stars didn't have to be as hardworking or as smart as their white counterparts and that people of other backgrounds might not also be born with great athletic gifts (and, for the record, the only pro golfer who can dunk a basketball, Dustin Johnson, happens to be white). One sportswriter, Steve Sailer, even speculated that the young Woods might be a superior genetic hybrid for combining the "muscularity and masculine charisma of an African-American superstar" with the "self-discipline and focus of the finest Asian-American athlete."[15] In this particular brand of speculative genetics and cultural criticism, Tiger made the case for an outbred family tree, and against the old taboo on interracial love and marriage.

Woods, clearly, raised the bar of strength and fitness in professional golf. His physical edge, however, derived from his rigorous training regimen, as opposed to some mystical genetic alchemy. In the old days, legends like Arnold Palmer and Jack Nicklaus smoked cigarettes on the course. Nicklaus was known as "Fat Jack" early on, and another top star, Billy Casper, earned the nickname "Jelly Belly." More than a few other touring pros carried a spare tire from too many cheeseburgers and lack of rigorous exercise. Gary Player, the mite-sized South African star, was regarded as an oddball fitness freak just for doing a few jumping jacks, push-ups, and squeezing a rubber ball now and then to strengthen his hands. By contrast, Tiger was the first top golfer with a reputation as a workout nut, making sure to find a gym everywhere he traveled. He spent countless hours on the practice range as well as in the weight room. Woods came to personify the new concept that golf demands fitness: a hard body trained to exacting golfing specifications. Now the typical professional golfer, if he hopes to hit the ball far and straight enough to compete, hires personal trainers and follows a regimen of diet and exercise along with extensive coaching with the latest computer and video equipment.

But what truly set Woods apart was his mind for the game. "Golf is ninety percent mental," as the longtime instructor Jim Flick puts it, "and the other ten percent is too." This does not mean you must possess a great intellect to be a top golfer. "I owe everything to golf," the journeyman pro Hubert Green once said. "Where else could a guy with an IQ as low as mine make so much money?" Golf does demand a special kind of confidence, composure, and concentration over the four or more hours it takes to play a round. Very little separates the physical skills of the top professionals, and it's willpower that has always marked the champions off from the rest. Nowhere is this clearer than in putting, those short little shots that normally account for almost half your score. Although practice and good form certainly help, putting requires no special physical ability. You could probably train a chimpanzee to do it. A professional golfer can make thirty or forty testy little three footers in a row on the practice green. Under pressure, however, it's not uncommon to see that same player "choke" or "suck air" on this same sort of short putt in the decisive final holes of a tournament. One thinks of Retief Goosen blowing one at the last hole of the 2001 U.S. Open or Mark Calcavecchia at the 1991 Ryder Cup. By contrast, Tiger never seemed to miss, no matter how high the stakes. He might sink thirty of thirty-one putts inside eight feet in a tournament, or sometimes every single one.

This cool under fire came partly from Tiger's upbringing. Earl, the former Green Beret, instilled an almost military discipline in his son through his training techniques. By Earl's own account, he pulled "every nasty, dirty, obnoxious trick" possible to improve his son's concentration, including coughing, dropping clubs, or starting up the golf cart in the middle of his swing.[16] Earl told Tiger that, because of this preparation, no one would be more mentally tough than he. It seemed to the golf world that the gruff and sometimes bombastic elder Woods had been right.

Tiger was never a huggable personality in the mold of some other sports superstars. His chief rival, the affable Phil Mickelson, would slap hands with the gallery, pose for pictures with fans, and sign

Earl Woods gives advice to the then nineteen-year-old Tiger at the Masters tournament, 1995. Courtesy of AP Wide World Photos.

autographs for little kids. Tiger invited no such affection, with his intimidating, unsmiling course demeanor. Many people assumed that his toughness came exclusively from Earl's boot-camp discipline. But Tiger told an interviewer that his dad was a "softie" compared to his mother. Tiger and Tida, as Kultida was nicknamed, were also extremely close, and yet he often said that she, and not Earl, was the one he was afraid of. "Old man is soft," Tida once said of Earl. "He cry. He forgive people. Not me. I don't forgive anybody." She taught her son to "step on the throats" of his competitors. "Asian

Elin Nordegren, Tiger Woods, and Kultida Woods at a charity event, 2006. L. Cohen/ WireImage/Getty Images.

woman is small, but dangerous, honey!," the barely-five-foot-tall Tida told the prominent golf journalist Jaime Diaz.[17] Tida and Earl never divorced, but they lived separately in the last decade or so before Earl's death, in 2006.

Like so many great athletes, Tiger seemed almost addicted to the thrill of competition. A friend of mine recalls being out on the practice putting green at the Duke University course one cold winter day. There was only one other golfer there, a tall man who soon sidled up to ask my friend if he wanted to have a putting contest. Strangers don't normally issue such practice green challenges, but my friend, a slight young English professor, noticed that the other man was Michael Jordan, the retired basketball legend. He agreed to the match and, happening also to be the friend who's a deadeye with his old Bullseye putter, promptly trounced his famous opponent. Woods was much like Jordan in relishing competition not just in his own sport, but also at ping-pong, cards, videogames, or any other contest. His friend and fellow touring professional, Notah Begay, once said that Tiger "hated to lose" more than any other golfer. A fierce joy in competing and coming out on top was a driving part of Woods's personality Although this ultra-competitiveness was part of what made Tiger such a great golfer, it could also come across as a bit childish and vindictive. "I love to compete," he told interviewer Ed Bradley on *Sixty Minutes*. "You and I could be playing cards right now, and I'd just want to kick your butt." Bradley, who was in his sixties and would die of cancer less than six months later, smiled, and yet seemed a bit taken aback. "You want to win?" he asked. "No," Tiger flashed a predatory smile, "I want to kick your butt. There's a difference."

Tiger's intensity and excellence intimidated opponents. According to a study conducted by a pair of economists, other pros averaged 48 strokes worse per round when they had to play with Woods, and those who actually had to play with the great star scored .48 higher. Those paired with Tiger during a tournament's pressure-packed final round scored almost a full shot worse than would have been otherwise expected.[18] The distracting large gallery that always followed Woods was part of the explanation. But Tiger's formidable aura was likely the bigger factor: the unsmiling stare, the powerful muscles, the fast and purposeful stride like some killer videogame robot (and his own EA Sports Tiger Woods golf game was a top-selling PlayStation, Xbox, and Wii attraction). Woods could go an entire round focused so ruthlessly on the task at hand that he sometimes wouldn't even speak to his playing partners.

Even Tiger's fans could be intimidated. When I joined the crowd of thousands following him at the U.S. Open tournament in 2004, I was struck by the nervousness, even fear, among the spectators about coughing or moving during his swing and being singled out for his withering displeasure. Tiger was like Apollo, a glorious yet frightening god. According to the philosopher Hans Ulrich Gumbrecht, sports fans want to imagine a distance between themselves and the star athlete great enough to believe that "their heroes inhabit a different world."[19] Woods did indeed seem from some other universe, with his divine skill and fierce focus. That child of the Brazilian slums, Edson Arantes do Nascimento (better known as Pelé), once described his own talents in a straightforward way: "God put Beethoven on the earth to create music; he made Michelangelo to paint; and he made me to play soccer."[20] The same, it seemed, could be said of Woods and golf.

The art of image management was also part of the Tiger Woods revolution. He contracted IMG to manage his affairs early in his career. This big company represents many Hollywood and sports stars and, as its website explains, "connects brands to global opportunities in sports, media, and entertainment." Everyone could see that Tiger was intense, brilliant, and charismatic with a golf club in his hand, and, as a brand, Tiger Woods stood for excellence and the pursuit of perfection. His advertisements for TAG Heuer, the pricey Swiss watch company, showed him following a shot in flight with the total concentration of a gem cutter faceting a precious diamond. Paradoxically, however, Americans tend to want their sports stars to be divine in ability, yet also to be the proverbial regular guy you might want to have a few beers with. If Tiger didn't seem very approachable on the golf course, his advertisers assured us that there was a more everyman Tiger away from the game. His commercials for Gillette showed him hamming it up in the locker room with fellow sports royalty Roger Federer and Thierry Henry, guys being guys. A spot for Buick featured an affable Tiger surprising and then mingling with weekend golfers as if to suggest that he enjoyed the company of the khaki-shorted and big-paunched golfing masses. A soulful embrace with Tida for American Express portrayed Tiger as a model of filial piety and human warmth. The truth or not of any of this was beside the point, for image was indeed everything in Tiger's case. He protected his privacy away from the game so tightly that most Americans knew very little about him aside from the steady stream of advertisements. Apparently as disciplined in his image management as in his golf game, Woods steered clear of anything

My name ...... *Tiger Woods* ......

childhood ambition *to beat dad in a game of golf*

last purchase *My friends new album from Beatle and the Blow fish*

indulgence ... *my boat*

biggest challenge *how can I become a better person tomorrow*

alarm clock *5:00AM sharp!!*

first job ..... *cart boy*

My life ..... *is hectic*

My card *is American Express)*

My life. My card.™

mylifemycard.com

Tiger and Kultida Woods embrace for *American Express* ad, 2006.

that might have slowed down the commercial juggernaut of his brand. He didn't Twitter, and he treated press-conference questions he didn't like with a cold stare and an abrupt "next question." He controlled the flow of information about his upcoming tournament appearances and family landmarks like his children's births through TigerWoods.com, the lavish "Official Web-Site of Tiger Woods."

By 2009, Woods was at an apogee of success and fame. His only problem seemed to be a bad left knee. Golf is normally the easiest of sports on the body. Artificial knees and hips do not keep older players from getting out for a round, and the "Wounded Warriors Project" has helped hundreds of war veterans with prosthetic arms and legs to take up the game. Besides the requisite bad backs and creaky joints among older players, it's freak accidents that seem to end or limit the careers of professional golfers (and, in fact, the great

Lee Trevino never quite recovered from being struck by lightning at the 1975 Western Open). But Tiger's left knee had to absorb the powerful torque from the follow through of his 120-mile-per-hour swing, many thousands and perhaps even millions of times over more than three decades. With typical reserve, the golfer and his camp did not reveal the injury's gravity. Woods entered the 2008 U.S. Open at San Diego's Torrey Pines with a torn anterior cruciate ligament and stress fractures in his left leg. He limped to victory in a playoff that was perhaps the single most riveting triumph of an already storied career.

Tiger had off-season surgery and spoke a few months later at a presidential inauguration gala for Barack Obama, with the whole Obama family in the audience. The Obama campaign had high-lighted their candidate's basketball skills, perhaps fearing he would come off as elitist should his penchant for golf be known. Obama jumped it up with the troops for the cameras and scrimmaged with several college teams. But, like almost all his predecessors, the forty-fourth president was also an avid golfer, escaping the White House on weekends for a round at Andrews Air Force Base and other local courses. It was fitting enough that Woods should have spoken at the Obama inauguration, because the two men were twin travelers in some uncanny ways. Both were the progeny of cross-racial, transnational marriages, Obama with his Kenyan father, Woods with his Thai mother. Each man had by dint of extraordi-nary talent and perseverance rocketed to the top of once whites-only professions—politics and golf—and become a global celebrity in the process. Some observers argued that Woods helped to pave the way for Obama's election by getting more white Americans accustomed to a high-achieving and seemingly trustworthy black man in com-mand. The January 2010 cover of *Golf Digest*, the game's most in-fluential magazine, featured an artist's simulation of the two men lining up a putt in some future round together (and they said they would plan one as soon as their schedules allowed). The accom-

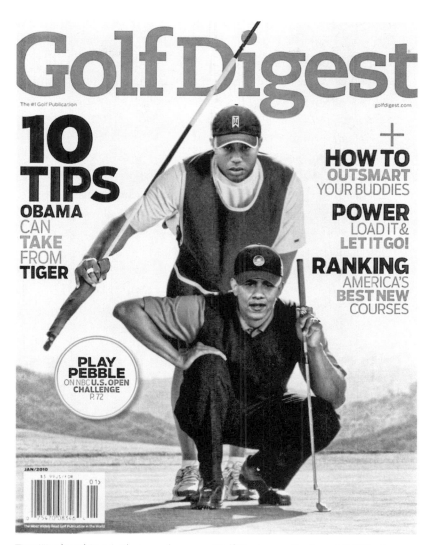

Tiger Woods and Barack Obama on the cover of *Golf Digest*, 2010. Courtesy of *Golf Digest*.

panying feature had "Ten Tips Obama Can Take from Tiger" and vice-versa. What the new president could supposedly learn from the golfer included "Cold Ferocity" and, Kultida's lesson, "How to Step on Their Necks." As for Tiger, it was suggested that the new president might teach him to "Dial It Back a Little," "Less Robot, More Warmth," and "The Art of Grace."

Woods's golfing success seemed to square with his personal life. Tiger and Elin had their second child, Charlie, just a few weeks after the presidential inauguration. Whether in a public relations ploy to burnish Tiger's image or just because the couple wanted to share its joy, the family released a series of relaxed, informal photographs of the growing Woods family. The pictures seemed to show a man who had it all: fame, riches, adoring blond wife, friendly family dogs, and now even the proverbial two kids. Tiger told reporters that "fatherhood was a dream come true." Despite the sleepless nights, he said, "I couldn't be happier than where I am right now."

And then came Thanksgiving night.

3

TIGERGATE, CELEBRITY SCANDAL, AND THE APOLOGY SOCIETY

The circumstances of Tiger's late-night accident seemed odd from the start. His mother, mother-in-law, Elin, and his two children had been gathered at the Woods house in the exclusive Isleworth gated community near Orlando for a family Thanksgiving. Why had Tiger driven off at 2 A.M.? How had he managed to crash his SUV just yards from his driveway? The police reports noted that Elin Woods had used a golf club to break the passenger-side window, then dragged her unconscious husband from the wreck. Woods had been ambulanced to the hospital with minor injuries and released a few hours later.

It did not take long for the news media and blogosphere to suggest that some sort of marital dispute had occurred. A week before the crash, the *National Enquirer* had reported a supposed extramarital affair between Woods and a New York nightclub hostess Rachel Uchitel, but the mainstream press had not picked up the story. As tabloid reporters and others now sought more details, Uchitel herself denied the *National Enquirer* report, but she later admitted to having been involved with Woods, at the last minute canceling the "press conference" where she was to divulge details. A website statement on TigerWoods.com tried to limit the damage, decrying "false, unfounded, malicious rumors." But it would subsequently be alleged that Tiger's camp had paid Uchitel a million dollars for her silence. The *Wall Street Journal* also later reported that Woods had made a secret deal to squelch an earlier *National Enquirer* story that would have included blurry 2007 photographs of his liaison, in an suv parked in a church lot, with a Florida waitress. According to the report, a conglomerate called American Media owned both the *National Enquirer* and *Men's Fitness*, and in return for the *Enquirer* story being scuttled, Tiger gave a long interview to and posed for the cover of *Men's Fitness*.[1]

After the crash, however, the tales of Tiger's infidelity could no longer be squelched. For several weeks, a new woman seemed to appear every day, many of them selling their stories of trysting with the golf superstar to the tabloids or television gossip shows. Each account seemed more sordid than the next. The diner waitress eventually gave details of her parking lot hook-up with Woods and various subsequent rendezvous at his Isleworth mansion; another woman said she'd had sex with him on the night his father died; and then there were the hundreds of "sexts" that the porn star Joslyn James posted on her website. Like many powerful men accustomed to having their way, Woods apparently imagined that he could do whatever he pleased without consequences. Several more Freudian-minded pundits suggested that, if only unconsciously, the golfer actually wanted to be caught so as to release himself from the burden of virtual perfection as an athlete, role model, and family man that being Tiger Woods had placed on him. Tiger had left such a trail of incriminating texts and voicemails to his lovers that it had become impossible to deny that he'd been sleeping around, no matter what his motivations.

As a sidebar, it also came out that Tiger's family life had never been as rosy as the image-makers had portrayed. In 2010 the journalist Tom Callahan published a book about Earl and Tiger suggesting that the originary mythology of a perfect, almost telepathic father-son bond had been only partly true.[2] While father and son had indeed been close, Earl had also been a notorious womanizer. According to Callahan (who also had good things to say about both Earl and Tiger), any "woman who came within fifty feet of Earl was a potential plaintiff."[3] The problem only worsened as the aging Woods took advantage of his celebrity as Tiger's father. Earl's skirt-chasing and marital infidelity had already begun to cause grief, tension, and family trouble when Tiger was still a boy. The younger Woods, a former high-school sweetheart recalled, would sometimes call in tears about his father having been with another woman. Earl had liked to boast that Tiger had inherited his toughness and will to win. The two, it seemed, had also been alike in their difficulty honoring their marriage vows. Tida, although she had no affection for her estranged husband, had acted as peacemaker between Earl and Tiger in Earl's last years, when tensions over Earl's latest trouble with a woman had estranged them for a stretch.

The prying tabloids, however, now focused on Tiger, and the story of his infidelity soon seemed to be everywhere. "Yes, He Cheated!," blared US in a cover story that promised to reveal the details of Tiger's "hotel hook-ups and dirty texts." As the literary theorist William Cohen notes, the coverage of a "scandal itself often becomes scandalous"—in other words, the media may find itself the target of backlash for the excesses of its own sensationalism.[4] In line with their self-styled profiles as serious news outlets, the likes of Newsweek, Time, and the New York Times maintained a certain ironic, soberly sociological distance in their Woods reporting. Newsweek, for example, pictured Tiger on its cover with the headline

"Why We Can't Look Away: Understanding Our Craven Celebrity Culture." This reportorial style allowed *Newsweek* and other outlets to have their cake and eat it too—they could sell copies to those interested in Tigergate's sordid details, yet simultaneously position themselves as more thoughtful and less bottom-feeding than the tabloid press. The result was to broadcast the beleaguered Tiger's troubles still more loudly into the echo chamber of American mass media and popular culture. *Vanity Fair* even published a spread of what it labeled "Tiger Woods's Inconvenient Women" in sex-kitten poses.

Letterman, Leno, and other mainline comedians made predictable hay of the revelation that, as one line had it, Woods was not a Tiger but a "cheetah." Tiger jokes went viral on the Internet, mostly lame or worse ("Tiger died and went to heaven for being such a great golfer; a day later, the pope also died. When he came through St. Peter's gates, the pope greeted Tiger and said how much he'd been looking forward to meeting the Virgin Mary. 'You're a day too late,' Tiger said"; "What's the difference between a golf ball and a car? Tiger Woods can drive a golf ball four hundred yards without hitting a tree"; and so on). Many would-be humorists played off the rumor that Elin Woods hadn't grabbed that golf club to break the window and rescue her husband, but instead to chase her adulterous husband from the house. "What do Tiger Woods and baby seals have in common?," one joke asked. "They've both been clubbed by Scandinavians." .

That Tiger was such a megacelebrity was only the most obvious reason that his serial philandering attracted such attention. Unfortunately for Woods, that year's end happened to be a slow news period, without any single big event like 9/11 or a stock-market crash to crowd out Tigergate. The shock-value quotient for the Tigergate story was also especially elevated, given the elements of revelation and surprise that are important variables in the algorithm of just how big a particular scandal will become. It wouldn't have been much of a story if a celebrity already notorious for womanizing had been caught sleeping around; but Tiger had been the mythical superstar beyond reproach. Film critic Richard Dyer suggests that part of scandal's attraction lies in seeming to reveal just what our heroes and heroines are "really like."[5] The curtain had been pulled back on Woods, and it appeared to expose the spotless, irreproachable, impregnable figure of Tiger as a hoax or at best a half-truth. And, of course, sex is always the *materia prima* for scandal in any event, and Tigergate was certainly a parable of the flesh, lust, and the perils of a wandering eye. We live in an America that loves booty-shaking videos, Hooters, half-naked cheerleaders, the Chippendale Dancers, Victoria's Secret, sex toys strip clubs, and every imaginable form of pornography (which garners more than a third of our Internet mouse clicks); yet this America also likes to finger wag and profess its adherence to the old Christian ideal of lifelong monogamy. Finally, too, there's the mentality that the behavioral economist Dan Ariely terms "herding."[6] As opposed to making their own decisions about what stories merit coverage, many media organizations follow the lead of others. That CNN, in particular, ran the story from the Thanksgiving car crash seemed to signal to every other news outlet that they should also report Tigergate. The torrent of coverage papered over the absurdity that the peccadilloes of a famous golfer should ever merit such media attention in the first place.

Tiger's world came apart. Several of his chief sponsors cut ties or halted ad campaigns involving the former corporate darling, among them TAG Heuer and, somewhat hypocritically, Accenture. (The consulting heavyweight had its own checkered history, having been, in its previous incarnation as the Arthur Andersen accounting firm, indicted for cooking the books in the Enron scandal.) The ubiquitous "Go On, Be a Tiger" airport billboards, which could now be read in a different way, came down almost overnight. One Internet joker had it that the only corporations still thinking about signing

Parody of Tiger Woods Nike ad, by an anonymous jokester, 2010.

Woods to an endorsement deal were Trojan, KY Jelly, Motel 6, Lava-life, Adultfriendfinder, and AshleyMadison. Others sampled and remixed some of Tiger's well-known commercials with a new sex spin. "Just Do Her" went one parody of his Nike ads. Woods himself disappeared from view. He was not seen in public for almost two months, and reportedly had entered a sex-addiction rehabilitation facility in Mississippi.

The subject of scandal has long fascinated anthropologists and other scholars. Back in the 1950s, Max Gluckman, the South African anthropologist, argued that gossip functions as a mechanism of solidarity and cohesion, discouraging African villagers from going beyond the limits of acceptable behavior by targeting them for censorious chatter.[7] Oscar Lewis, Gluckman's American contemporary, took a darker view based on his research in Mexico, suggesting that rumor only rips local society apart.[8] Unlike gossip in these more tra-

d_tional worlds, the hallmark of more modern scandal is its circulation by the means of mass communication. Early American mani-
festos and pamphlets already spread dirt about leading politicians
in the era of the founding fathers. Thomas Jefferson, for example,
used broadsheets to deride his sometime friend John Adams as a
mentally unstable monarchist, and, in turn, Adams circulated reports that Jefferson was an "intriguer" whose Declaration of Inde-
pendence was "unoriginal" (and one can only speculate about how
Jefferson's enemies might have exploited his secret interracial romance with Sally Hemmings).

Now scandal has become a multibillion dollar industry. Talk
shows and trash television, glossy magazines, supermarket tabloids,
and gossip blogs power this vast and viral entertainment complex,
with the daily newspapers, newsweekly magazines, and other more
respectable media joining in to comment on and further amplify
the biggest scandals, just as they did with Tigergate. Film theorists
Adrienne Maclean and David Cook suggest that modern scandals
can be subdivided into three overlapping categories.[9] The generic
psychodrama features ordinary people enmeshed in extraordinary,
often freakish, and sometimes less-than-verifiable situations ("Baby
Born with Two Heads," "Bigfoot Was My Nanny," and so forth). By
contrast, the institutional scandal involves the malfeasance of government officials, business leaders, or corporations in the classic
mold of Watergate, Iran-Contra, and Enron. Tiger's troubles fit into
the very large third slot, namely the celebrity scandal, with its focus
on the misdeeds of the rich and famous. A child of Hollywood and
the movie industry, the celebrity scandal dates back to the original American tabloids of the pre-Second World War years and their
chronicling of movie-star foibles, with encouragement from major
studios wanting to increase public interest in their actors. We have
also witnessed what might be called the 'celebritization" of politicians and sports stars, and their lives have provided more fodder
for the tattling tabloids and the blogosphere. As John Edwards, Bill

Clinton, and too many others to name have discovered, the womanizing, drinking, or other excesses of presidents and star athletes are no longer off-limits in America's new culture of exposure (and in contrast to a less puritanical Europe, where the extramarital affairs of powerful men draw little commentary). If anything, American politicians and sports heroes now find themselves held to a more exacting standard of honesty, fair play, and rectitude than other celebrities. A lusty libertinism when it comes to sex, drink, or drugs seems almost requisite for a certain kind of high-living musician or movie star. Eminem, Bono, or Fifty Cent sleeping around wouldn't have set off anything like the same explosion of coverage as Tigergate in the wacky modern tabloid calculus of merit and opprobrium.

The threshold for surprise and condemnation, it should be noted, varies depending on the sport. It's not necessarily big tabloid news when a star from a more rough-and-tumble, testosterone-laden game like football, baseball, boxing, soccer, or basketball cheats on his wife. But golf has always placed a special premium on honor and good sportsmanship. You're supposed to maintain a respectful, church-like silence every time your playing partner is about to hit a shot. A dress code bans professional golfers from wearing shorts in keeping with the game's gentlemanly—some would say stuffy—conventions of etiquette and propriety. And golf is the only sport where you're on your honor to penalize yourself for any rules violation. At the 1925 U.S. Open, the legendary amateur star Bobby Jones famously called a two stroke penalty on himself for accidentally moving the ball a fraction of an inch with his club, even though no one else saw the infraction. That penalty cost Jones the championship. As for Tiger, he was certainly not the first golf star to have extramarital escapades. The magnetic Arnold Palmer, among others, had reportedly been known as a bit of a Don Juan in his younger years, but his indiscretions had been kept quiet.[10] In today's brave new world of predatory media reporting on private celebrity lives, by contrast, everyone from Abu Dhabi and Budapest to Zanzibar knew about Tiger's indiscretions. That he was a golfer—given the game's staid tradition of probity, rectitude, and a button-down moral conservatism—added yet another twist of scandalousness to the noxious cocktail of voyeurism, speculation, and indignation that was Tigergate.

The cultural critic Laura Kipnis may, in fact, be right in declaring that celebrity scandal has become America's favorite national spectator sport.[11] Whether Lindsay Lohan's latest rehab plans or some new sign of trouble in Brangelina's marriage, a good scandal's pleasure lies not only in having concealed truths exposed, but also in the drama itself and its capacity to evoke a whole range of emotions, whether outrage, curiosity, sympathy, amusement, fascination, or incredulity. Ours is also a society that relishes the opportunity to pass judgment and the accompanying sense of power and moral righteousness. Millions log on to yelp.com, tripadvisor.com, and other such rating sites, which let you play the critic, complete with numerical ratings. We've taken over the judging entirely in television shows in the "American Idol" mold, where texted votes determine the outcome (oddly, it's only for what one might consider the more consequential matter of electing public officials that Americans somehow have trouble making it to the polls). The celebrity scandal puts the rich and famous in the docket. We are given still another opportunity to weigh evidence, come to a decision, and make that opinion known, whether in the water-cooler conversation or on an Internet comment board. Gossip websites offer dozens of interactive polls, sometimes dosed with a catty irony, just for the fun of it. StyleHive.com allowed you to register your verdict on the "biggest fashion disaster of 2010," with choices including Rihanna's "Ronald McDonald look" and Lady Gaga's skirt-steak dress.

Most of us wouldn't mind being celebrities ourselves, or at least a bit richer and more famous. We can now text in our blurry cell-phone photographs and sightings of movie idols and other stars to TMZ.com or *Entertainment Weekly*, just like genuine paparazzi. As many pundits have noted, Facebook even allows us to make celebrities of ourselves, complete with fans, followers, candid photographs, sightings, and status updates about our personal lives. But it's not exactly the real thing. We know that movie stars, football heroes, and their ilk are a different breed—more good-looking, wealthy, desired, well-dressed, or talented than most of us will ever be. Scandal is a democratic leveler, cruel for celebrities and comforting for us. Here we find reassurance that the chosen ones have the same awful, tawdry, painful woes and secrets as the rest of us. It's not always exactly Schadenfreude, or "joy in harm," as the word's German etymology has it, and yet the woes of the rich, famous, and powerful seem to reverse the arrow by putting them at the mercy of our judgment, our Internet polls, our forgiveness. And we get something to talk about in the checkout line or in the chat room in the bargain.

Sociologist Herman Gray notes how scandal has sometimes served to enforce racial boundaries and hierarchies.[12] The saga of a very early celebrity athlete, the heavyweight boxing champion Jack Johnson, was a case in point. A child of former slaves, Johnson thrilled crowds with his showmanship, skill, and mind for the ring. His victory over James Jeffries, the legendary former champion who had promised to reclaim the title for "the white race," was one of the most publicized sporting events of the early twentieth century. The fearless, flamboyant Johnson refused to obey the taboo on interracial marriage; all three of his wives were white. This scandalized many white observers (and some prominent black leaders, like Booker T. Washington, who also believed in "race conservation") and led to Johnson's conviction, under the Mann Act, for "transporting women across state lines for immoral purposes."[13] Love, or even flirtation, between a black man and a white woman was, after all, the great American taboo, and the main cause of lynching in the Jim Crow South. Johnson spent a year in Leavenworth federal prison. He died several years later, in a car crash, racing away from a North Carolina diner that had refused to serve him because he was black. By a more reasonable definition, as Gray notes, the dictates of Jim Crow might have been labeled the real scandal, but it was Johnson's violation of the taboo against "miscegenation" that provoked outrage—a prime example of scandal being deployed to enforce discrimination and bigotry.

By the time of Tiger Woods, almost a century later, the nexus between race and scandal had changed. No longer, in the post-civil-rights-movement era, could the media or anyone in the public eye get away with making directly derogatory racial comments. A first prominent casualty of the changing standards was Secretary of Agriculture Earl Butz, who resigned after telling a noxious n-word joke. Al Campanis became the first well-known sports figure to lose his job for racist comments, the ones about blacks lacking "necessities" required to become baseball managers. Only a few years ago, shock jock Don Imus was fired for his repellent would-be joke that members of the Rutgers women's basketball team were "nappy-headed h-s."[14] The new expectation for sensitivity has extended by now to other markers, like gender, sexual orientation, and age. A CBS golf commentator, Ben Wright, lost his job in 1995 for suggesting that lesbians on the women's tour "give the game a bad image" and that women would never excel at golf because "their boobs get in the way." Nowadays in short, derogatory comments have themselves become scandalous; most announcers and sports stars have become smart enough to avoid them.

The contrast between the coverage of Jack Johnson and Tiger Woods dramatically illustrated the changed atmosphere. Like Jack Johnson, Tiger married a white woman. His wedding ceremony was featured in *People*, *Entertainment Tonight*, and other media outlets high and low, yet—in a reflection of the change in views across the decades—not a negative word appeared about this interracial union, and, in fact, the coverage avoided the matter of race and color altogether, covering the marriage as just another celebrity wedding. The only disappointment for reporters was that they were denied access to the Barbados ceremony itself, with its guest list of American royalty, which included Oprah Winfrey, Bill Gates, and Michael Jordan. All the public got were some blurry paparazzi photos and stray leaked details, like the fact that the planners had ordered five hundred roses in red and black, the colors that Tiger wears in each tournament's final round. It was a long way from newspaper editorials that had denounced Jack Johnson as "the black bugaboo of the prize ring" for his "ill-assorted" relationships with women from the "superior race."[15]

The media also shied away from race and the touchy topic of intermarriage in covering Tigergate. Although intermarriage has more than doubled since 1980, surveys show that millions of Americans remain uncomfortable with cross-racial relationships (and, apparently less adventurous in this respect, women are more likely than men to declare a preference for racial endogamy). More than forty years have now passed since the first televised interracial kiss, between Lieutenant Uhuru and Captain Kirk, on the Starship Enterprise, and yet it is still considered a bit edgy for magazine catalogs or television programs to show a black man and a white woman kissing or even holding hands. Every single one of Tiger's known trysts were with white women, but once again the newspapers, television shows, and magazines altogether ignored the subject of race and color. While tabloids like the *National Enquirer*, *Globe*, and *Star* take everything from weight to hairstyle and taste in clothes as fair game for comment and criticism, even these most voracious predators in the media food chain stay away from the electric third rail of racial identity and cross-racial desire, in accordance with early-twenty-first-century protocol.

Tigergate itself seemed, in fact, to follow what has become the very generic playbook for celebrity scandal. Once outed for bad behavior, a celebrity can deny the charges or try to ignore the bad press. The most common strategy, however, is now to offer some sort of public apology. In an older day, very few prominent figures, especially men, would even have considered making a statement of contrition for their failings; it would have been unmanly and a bit odd to do so. But the apology has become a staple in twenty-first-century reconciliation politics and image management. It was in the era after the Second World War that peoples and nations began through expressions of contrition to seek forgiveness for past crimes. Thus, for example, the United States government apologized to Japanese Americans for their wartime internment; the British Crown apologized to Australian aborigines for the brutalities of conquest; and so forth. What might be termed "social apologies" accompanied the rise of the individual mea culpa in politics, sports, and other fields. Richard Nixon was a godfather of the genre, with his Checkers speech, in the early 1950s. While the speech was not exactly an apology, it created a template by which disgraced politicians could seek forgiveness to save their careers, in Nixon's case through the maudlin vehicle of his "little cocker spaniel dog." By the 1990s, famous figures routinely confessed their sins to try to win back public affections. Bill Clinton expressed televised contrition for the Monica Lewinsky affair; the New York governor Eliot Spitzer apologized for hiring prostitutes; the Yankees slugger Alex Rodriguez declared remorse for his use of performance-enhancing drugs; and there are far too many others to name. Top public-relations firms often recommended apology, whether heartfelt or for show, as the best celebrity strategy for damage management; they scheduled press conferences and appearances on the *Oprah Show*, in interviews with Barbara Walters, or on *Sixty Minutes* for their clients to come clean. To seek the public's forgiveness played to the Christian ideal of mercy for the repentant sinner, and to the great American ideology of second chances. As demonstrated by the return to prominence of such formerly disgraced celebrities as the decorating doyenne Martha Stewart (who was jailed for insider trading) and the star quarterback Michael Vick (who served time for dogfighting), the tactic of apology could be effective, especially when paired with other gestures of repentance. So common did the apology become, however, that many Americans developed a certain bored cynicism, as suggested by the title of an anthology published in 2006: *My Bad: 25 Years of Public Apologies and the Appalling Behavior that Inspired Them*.[16]

Tiger posted a sanitized expression of regret on his website. But the protocol now demands that an apology be delivered publicly, with this ritualized humiliation being the price for a chance at forgiveness. At last, Woods went before the cameras in February, three months after his crash. Only his mother, a few friends and golf officials, and some reporters were allowed to be there, but all three major networks broke away to cover the fourteen-minute statement, as if it were some major presidential announcement. Woods had hired, in fact, the public-relations firm run by George W. Bush's former press secretary, and it likely helped him prepare his text. When golfing, Tiger had always been in fearless control. Now he looked nervous and vulnerable; he seemed to have aged quite suddenly as well, looking more like his father Earl (who had died of cancer three years before). The "Gentle Path" program at the Pine Grove addiction facility, where Woods had been in treatment, follows the twelve-step model made famous by Alcoholics Anonymous. Apparently guided by these principles in his statement, Woods took full responsibility for his troubles, acknowledging that his behavior had been out of control and listing all those that he had hurt, from Elin to his mother and sponsors. His statement was tightly and strategically scripted toward the eventual rehabilitation of his image. But it was also eloquent and self-lacerating in ways that were compelling to some who watched (and I myself was moved, even though I recognized what a dodgy carnival Tigergate was in the first place). A cartoon depicted Tiger as the gold medalist in a competition for "Best Apology for Cheating on Wife," beating out Bill Clinton and the South Carolina governor Mark Sanford. A *Washington Post* columnist praised the statement as revealing the "real" Tiger: before, this

Tiger Woods, Bill Clinton, and Mark Sanford in competition, by Mike Luckovich, 2010. By permission of Mike Luckovich and Creators Syndicate, Inc.

line of reasoning went, there was the wholesome corporate pitchman; then the selfish sex maniac; and now something more human, the flawed hero struggling to keep his life together. Others were more skeptical. "He is actually sorry," commented harmony1128 on the CNN website, "for losing millions of dollars in the last 3 months."

It was unclear what Elin Woods made of it all. The scripting of scandal leaves the wronged wife a very limited menu of choices. She can choose to stick with the unfaithful husband in the way of Hillary Clinton and many others, or break up with him, which is more rare. Only a short time before the Woods scandal hit the headlines, Jennifer Sanford, the wife of the wayward South Carolina governor, became a minor postfeminist heroine by booting Sanford and filing for divorce. Elin Woods, the daughter of a former Swedish government minister, had always been something of a mystery, having never given a single interview. She was conspicuous by her absence at Tiger's apology, and yet she had not yet left him. Tiger himself noted in his statement that Elin wanted more than expressions of remorse. "As she pointed out to me," Woods said, "my real apology to her will not come in the form of words. It will come from my behavior over time." It was very strange to see such a kingly, unimpeachable figure as Woods reduced to such an abject state.

4

INTERNET WARS, SEX ADDICTION, AND
THE CRUCIFIXION OF TIGER WOODS

I read a small library of books in trying to make sense of Tigergate. Many observers, anthropologists and not, point to how scandal may be manipulated, sometimes manufactured to serve political ends. According to political scientist James Scott, surreptitious talk about real or imagined misbehavior by the powerful can sometimes even become a "weapon of the weak," a way to destabilize the ruling order without the costs of more open rebellion.[1] A well-known case comes from the lead-up to the French Revolution. As much as or more than the high-minded new Enlightenment ideals of democracy and freedom, discontent with ancien régime spread through whispered slander, libelous songs, and *nouvelles à la main*, broadsheets that were the forerunners of the modern supermarket tabloid. Reports about Marie Antoinette fornicating with farm animals and other tales of purported aristocratic debauchery heated demands for revolutionary change.[2] Gossip may also serve the strong, of course. Whether as a true believer or a rank opportunist, billionaire Donald Trump proclaimed himself a "birther" when testing the waters for a presidential bid.[3] These mostly conservative conspiracy theorists propagated the shaggy dog story that Barack Obama was not born in the United States and thus was ineligible for the presidency.[4]

The Tiger Woods scandal presented no obvious connection to affairs of state, and yet it nonetheless plugged into trends, concerns, and anxieties far beyond the golf world. As a would-be digital-age anthropologist, albeit with the crude computer skills of one who learned to type on a manual Olivetti, I found the Internet an especially productive place for learning more about the strong feelings that Tiger's troubles evoked. My research into golf culture had begun in much more conventional fashion. I recorded dozens of interviews with club pros, equipment designers, black golf pioneers, retired caddies, and many others to learn more about the ins and outs of the game. Ever since the era of Bronislaw Malinowski in the Trobriand Islands, before the Second World War, the cornerstone of anthropology has been fieldwork, in particular the practice of going to live among the people we want to study so as to immerse ourselves in their way of life (ironically, Malinowski himself little enjoyed his Trobriand sojourn, and his diary complained of the heat, confided lust for island women, and derided the natives with racial epithets). This "participant-observation"—or "deep hanging out," in more colloquial terms—used to entail moving into the proverbial native village for some extended time period to learn the local language and customs. Like other such sprawling contemporary topics, golf requires a more mobile research strategy. To this end, I visited a club-manufacturing factory in Taiwan, an experimental turf-grass farm in North Carolina, and various other locales. The closest I came to "participant-observation"—admittedly no great sacrifice in the service of science—was going out to play golf myself. I'd pair up with strangers and in the process learn more about the game and those that find themselves drawn to it. I was never quite sure what my playing partners made of the little notebook I'd sometimes pull out of my golf bag.

I followed Tigergate through the mainstream media. But now I also had at my disposal a whole new trove of material, namely the commentary about the scandal on the Internet. From chat rooms at sites like Hollywood Gossip and the ubiquitous TMZ.com to the comments section at the websites for ESPN, *Ebony*, and the *New York Times*, literally tens of thousands of people weighed in at the tale's every twist. That I should find myself looking to the Internet to understand sentiment about Tigergate is not unusual, for anthropologists nowadays often do so. We have a growing assortment of ethnographies about different dimensions of cyberspace, all conducted primarily through virtual fieldwork, as opposed to meeting people face-to-face, much less going to live with them. Tom Boellstorff, for example, created the avatar "Tom Bukowski" to research a book about Second Life, a popular online virtual world.[5] His "participant-observation" included bar hopping, buying property and building a house, and attending music concerts and other activities. So relatively common has virtual research become that one younger anthropologist refers tongue-in-cheek to old-style face-to-face fieldwork as "off-line ethnography."[6]

My research was limited to reading Internet commentary, and only a fraction of the gigantic, far-flung collection of posts at that. Some scholars have described how people join Second Life, Perfect World, or World of Warcraft to invent a "second self," a whole new "life on the screen" for themselves, in the words of sociologist Sherry Turkle.[6] And so-called trollers have been known to post intentionally provocative comments just for the fun of watching the trouble it stirs up.[7] But the web is also a platform for airing our own very personal views, not just those of some virtual alter ego. It's part primal group-therapy session, part town meeting where anyone can get up to have their say, with the twist that you can remain anony-

Tiger Woods Crucified by the Press, by Daryl Cagle, 2010. Courtesy of Daryl Cagle.

mous if you wish. As everyone knows, millions of Americans ex-
ploit that anonymity to write things in their posts that they'd never
dare to say openly or to anyone's face. In the case of Tigergate, I
found that the comments, posts, and chats revealed views about the
touchy matters of race, sex, and the body that remain very powerful
in America, yet too politically incorrect for most people to be brave
or foolish enough to voice without concealing their real names.
All manner of prejudice, bigotry, and sometimes sheer weirdness
gushed to the surface for me, as the curious and sometimes puzzled
anthropologist, to try to decipher.

Consider the flap over the cartoonist Daryl Cagle's caricature of
Woods crucified. Worshipful golf announcers had often repeated
clichés about Tiger's "passion" for the game. That term, with the
golfing Casanova's libidinousness exposed, now had a double meaning. Adding a third sense to the passion of Tiger Woods, the cartoon

cast Tiger as the protagonist of those Easter Week passion plays that depict Christ's stations of the cross, from death sentence to tomb. In this rendering, the media is performing the crucifixion, the traditional tenth stop on the Via Dolorosa. In Cagle's thinly veiled allegory, a scrawny reporter pokes Tiger in the ribs with a golf club, just as the Roman soldier had jabbed the suffering Christ.

One might or might not agree with the cartoon's premise that the media was persecuting Tiger, but the comment thread on cartoonist Daryl Cagle's website took another path, namely into the exegesis of Christ's life and the perennial American debate about freedom of religion and the press. One poster, Fred, thought that the cartoonist had misinterpreted the bible: "According to scripture," he wrote, "Jesus of Nazareth was crucified albeit without sin. Mr. Woods has admitted to sin. The difference is profound and negates the point of your cartoon." Black Tantalus disagreed: "To be historical, Jesus was killed by Italians for being a Jew doing Jewy things; sin or no sin was not a consideration; sedition against the Roman government was." (In the grand tradition of anthropological attention to local detail, I have reproduced the misspellings, strange punctuation, free-style grammar, and other orthographic idiosyncrasies typical of Internet commentary in the age of texting and instant messaging.)[8] But Call Me Conservative opined that Cagle, the cartoonist, had blasphemed by drawing Tiger as Jesus at all: "The reference to Tiger being hung in the form of Jesus is offensive to Christians who practice their faith and revere their Lord and Savior." This provoked a tirade, from Lexington, against "overzealous, bible-thumping, unhealthily-addicted-to-the-Jesus-fetish Christians." Several other posters, in turn, clarified that they did not object to the cartoon's publication, but insisted on their own freedom of speech to declare it inappropriate. "We do not have the freedom to force Cagle to remove this cartoon," said Susan, "but we do have the freedom to dislike it and tell him why." A global controversy over a cartoon of Muhammad, including death threats against the Danish cartoonist, had occurred not long before. Susan positioned herself as a believer in religion and free speech, in contrast to either the more bible-thumping Christianity of Call Me Conservative or fundamentalist Islam. Here Tigergate became an unlikely forum for theology and politics, and, more broadly, signaled just how much religion still matters in an America that surveys indeed show has become more religious in recent decades. It wasn't clear whether any of the posters realized that Tiger himself had been raised a Buddhist by Tida. His apology had included an expression of regret for having "drifted away" from Buddhist teachings and the belated promise to be more faithful to the Buddhist teaching "that a craving for things outside ourselves causes an unhappy and pointless search for security."

Virtual reaction to Tiger's troubles also opened, less surprisingly, a debate about sex, love, and marriage. Americans idealize marriage, down to the flowers and bridal dresses, expensive ceremonies and declarations of eternal love, yet we are very bad at it. Recent surveys show that more than 60 percent of married men and 50 percent of married women have had at least one affair; 54 percent of newlyweds will divorce within fifteen years. Indeed, America has the world's highest divorce rate, Russia a distant second. Many posters nonetheless announced their disappointment with Woods, usually expressing sympathy for Elin. On ESPNConversations, a message board administered by the ubiquitous sports network, imjustrich voiced this view: "I know I don't want my son to look up to somebody who had affairs with what 14#### stars and devestated his own beautiful wife in the process." A female friend of mine, a golfer good enough to have played on her high-school men's team, explained that she'd admired Tiger because he seemed so true to his wife and kids, "the last of the good guys" in her words. She was sad and a bit disgusted to learn that Woods had been so callous about breaking his marriage vows.

Such reactions recall the cultural critic Lauren Berlant's concept of the "female complaint." According to this view, many twenty-first-century American women feel disappointed by the "the tenuous relation of romantic fantasy to lived intimacy."[9] Everything from Harlequin novels to television and movies push romantic, heterosexual, monogamous love as an achievable ideal, even though the evidence of our own lives often suggests otherwise, and the tabloids reporting the latest celebrity infidelity only reinforce a sense of the precariousness of it all. But Berlant also notes that women may "take tremendous pleasure" in following "how other women manage."[10] The likes of *People* and *US*, in fact, gave constant updates about how Elin was coping. ("Still angry and facing more humiliation," *People* reported on its cover, "Tiger's wife weighs the ultimate question: keep him or dump him?") Another reason Tigergate had such traction was that it drew attention from both the more manly domain of sports fandom and its more female counterpart of celebrity-lifestyle followers, a crossover extravaganza with something for both sexes in this sense.

Many Internet posters seemed most disturbed by the hypocrisy of what they now perceived to have been Tiger's selling of a false image. Tarquinis1 compared Woods to an infamous Ponzi schemer: "He professionally marketed himself to a worldwide audience as much more than a talented athlete but as a decent man, a family man who loved his wife and children. . . . Just how is this fundamentally different from Bernie Madof [sic]? Professionally marketed frauds, for the sake of a literal ocean of financial reward." The ideals of honesty and authenticity define the archetypal American male hero in the mold of George Washington to Gary Cooper and John Wayne. Many of Tiger's former fans believed he had fallen altogether from the pantheon. They saw the golfer now as a "sexual psycho," "uber cad," or as in one poster's thesaurus of invective, "arrogant, spoiled, bad tempered, childish, immature, foul-mouthed, whiny, disloyal, condescending, infantile. repugnant, loathsome, abominable, detestable, offensive, despicable, abhorrent and damnable." As writer Maggie Quale notes, the "line between audience and celebrity" has become more porous, in an age where we know so much more about the private lives of the rich and famous.[11] We speak of Brad, Beyoncé, A-Rod, and Tiger, using their first names as if they were personal friends. The intimacy that Americans feel with their celebrities may account for the almost personal sense of betrayal and fury in the reaction to Tiger's indiscretions (with Internet anonymity and what has been called its "culture of sadism" permitting such venting without consequences).

In his televised apology, which garnered half a million hits on YouTube alone, Tiger readily admitted to his "irresponsible and selfish behavior." But Woods also made reference to his "treatment" at the Mississippi program and in the process introduced the topic of sex addiction into the discussion. That this term now exists suggests the power of the addiction model in the American zeitgeist today. The concept of addiction reconfigures patterns of behavior once conceived of as individual moral failings into "diseases" that demand systematic intervention and treatment to enable "recovery." Alcohol was the model's original, but the notion of addiction has since gone viral and is now applied to smoking, narcotics, gambling, overeating, videogames, sex, and even shopping. To borrow from anthropologists Didier Fassin and Richard Rechtman, we have become an "empire of addiction."[12] Alcoholics Anonymous, the brainchild of New York stockbroker Bill Wilson during the Great Depression, established the famous twelve-step program for treating addiction through individual responsibility, group support, and spiritual awakening (the third step is to turn "our lives over to God as we understand him"). Every week, more than ten million people worldwide attend meetings of Alcoholics and Narcotics Anonymous alone, despite Sid Vicious's famous declaration that "rehab is for quitters."

Most Americans, pace Vicious, accept the concepts of drug and alcohol addiction. These seem to have a tangible biochemical explanation. As for sex addiction, the website for Sex Addicts Anonymous suggests that you may be one if you have "powerlessness over addictive sexual behavior" with "resulting unmanageability" of your life. It was possible to argue that Tiger fit this description. His liaisons seemed compulsive in their manic frequency, and they certainly made his life unmanageable. The PGA tour commissioner Tim Finchem, who wanted his biggest draw back on the tour, was happy enough to play along. "We need to be supportive of him," he told the *Golf Channel*, "and whatever he wants to do." Others were far more skeptical. "You're a sex addict," posted imkoma on one message board. "Please!!!!!!! What a cowardly excuse Tiger. . . . Grow a pair & man up you little wuss." "The only help Tiger Woods needs," added BornAgain1984 from a more moralizing Christian standpoint, "is stop his selfish and egotistical desires to please himself and begin thinking about the needs of his wife and children." These reactions were not altogether fair. Tiger may have claimed addiction, yet he blamed only himself in his apology, in accordance with the twelve-step method. This system, also the magna carta for Sex Addicts Anonymous, requires from its followers "a searching and fearless moral inventory" and "making amends" to "all persons we [have] harmed." But the criticism of Tiger indicated larger American doubts about the very idea of sex addiction. Many of us, including me, had not even heard of the concept until Tiger spoke of it, and its mention tends to elicit some combination of snarky laughter, eye-rolling, and derision. Isn't sleeping around a failure to rein in the id, not a disease? The concept of sex addiction has remained a hard sell, no matter that Sex Addicts Anonymous claims thousands of members.[13]

Tiger's defenders, mostly male by appearances, sometimes resorted to a biological explanation of another kind. "Sorry to all," posted Andreas on the *Hollywood Gossip* comment board. "All men just do that. It is our nature. Women will never understand that. It has nothing to do with respect, fidelity or religion. It is the man's nature to be polygamous." Travis made the same case and, like a number of posters, flipped the blame to Elin through the misogynist image of the castrating, ball-busting wife: "Go tiger, don't care about what they said, having several girls is male nature. And they don't care if they are shared. Just that Sweden b———. Losers go to church." Not everyone agreed. Melmel contributed to the same raunchy *Hollywood Gossip* thread: "For all the men on here that are saying that its 'nature' for a man to just cheat you can all just suck each others d****!!!! Because all you men know that if your wife cheated with that many men you would call her every name in the book and want to kill yourselves for it!!!!" But this was the minority position on this particular message board. "What he has done it is not NEW," said rosi of Tiger. "ALL MEN have the animal in them." Here, the supposed animality of the Y-chromosome was adduced to explain men cheating. For many decades now, feminist theorists have sought to show that differences in male and female behavior have more to do with upbringing, expectations, and other cultural factors than any preprogrammed biological reasons. A large body of scholarship also now demonstrates how the invocation of supposedly innate differences in ability and temperament between groups of people has been used to justify the oppression of women and people of color, among others. None of this seems to have slowed the circulation of various brands of crude determinism that take a caricature of biology as destiny.

Others took to the Internet with the more libertarian position that the superstar's personal life was his own business. These posters shared the belief that Tigergate and other such celebrity scandals were just "pseudoevents" in the historian Daniel Boorstin's famous term.[14] They directed their anger not at Tiger, but the media for devoting so much attention to his sex life. Typical was a thread on the ABC News/Entertainment website (the slashed name itself an indicator of the blurred boundary between traditional news and gossip fluff in twenty-first-century "infotainment"). "When did ABC become a gossip rag?," wondered sensible99: "Leave this story to the national Enquirer and TMZ. It's time the media got back on track and start reporting the news." Many agreed with Jimof1913:

"The only ones he [Tiger] owes an apology to are his wife, his kids, his family, and her family. Who does owe me an apology? The media who thinks everybody wants or cares about this." The *Washington Post* draws an older, more educated, and politically liberal readership, and B202 offered a more developed critique of the Tigergate coverage: "We never faced ourselves after the Big Lie that was Vietnam. We never faced ourselves after the Big Lie that was Iraq. But we know ALL ABOUT Tiger Woods' sex life. God help us with this media running the show. Scum is too polite a word to capture it." Mpowered also invoked the trope of codependency between the mass media and the public in a conspiracy of ignorance and denial: "What a short attention span, misplaced moral outrage and listing ethical compass the American public displays through an enabling media machine time and time again."

Cynicism about the media's role dates back to the earliest years of modern mass communication. Max Horkheimer and Theodor Adorno, Marxist critics of the so-called Frankfurt School in pre-Second World War Germany, saw how Hitler manipulated the newspapers, radios, and the newer medium of film to bolster Nazism. They viewed the "culture industry" of mass media in both Nazi Germany and American capitalism as an instrument for creating a passive, one-dimensional citizenry unable to think for itself.[15] Noam Chomsky, the famed linguist turned left-wing guru, argues that today's mainstream media has become a "propaganda machine" for "manufacturing consent" with the malfeasance of greedy multinational corporations and American adventurism abroad. The likes of B202 and Mpowered stood very much in this critical tradition, in lambasting the media for turning Tigergate into such a big story. They saw it as a red herring, a distraction from anything like the real news in the *panem et circenses* fashion of the Roman Caesars. "The difference," said John14 on the *Washington Post* board, in reference to hunger and unemployment in America today, "is that the Romans at least also provided bread."

Of course, you could also be critical of the critics. The Slovenian intellectual and provocateur extraordinaire Slavoj Žižek, in fact, questions whether seeing through the smokescreen of the "propaganda machine" means much at all.[16] To think you see the truth behind justifying ideology is a false freedom, according to Žižek, because the modern capitalist system thrives on cynicism and irony; it does not need to cloak itself in mystifying mythologies of any kind. Even the world's leftist critics, after all, still normally go to the mall, pay their taxes, and otherwise engage with the "life processes" that sustain the global world order. The illusion is to think you can live without illusions, according to Žižek. Those outraged at the attention devoted to Tigergate imagined themselves to be clear-sighted seers as against the more ignorant masses who bought into the false premise that the scandal was worth following in the first place. They were only playing a role in a puppet theater of truth, cynicism, and ideology, if Žižek has it right (and I'd like to think that matters aren't quite altogether as hopeless as this particular globe-trotting academic superstar would have us believe).

No such doubts troubled B202. He followed his first post with a second broadside against the *Washington Post*, for foregrounding "this utterly irrelevant tabloid drivel story" that seemed to draw more column space than the wars in Iraq and Afghanistan.

"A million deaths," he ended. "A billion new enemies for America. A trillion dollars in debt. And you are all over the story of some golfer who for some reasons thinks he owes me an apology."

"Sorry. I'm not that co-dependent."

5

POSTRACIAL FANTASIES,

RACIAL REALPOLITIK

The fuss over Tigergate also reopened the old question of Tiger's racial identity. As part of educating his son, Earl had told Tiger about life under Jim Crow and how he, the lone black player on the Kansas State baseball team, could not stay in the same hotels as his teammates or eat with them. Tiger himself was early on exposed to the realities of racism and discrimination. According to a story he related for his friend Charles Barkley's book *Who's Afraid of a Large Black Man?* "I became aware of my racial identity on my first day of school, on my first day of kindergarten. A group of sixth graders tied me to a tree, spray-painted the word 'n——' on me, and threw rocks at me. That was my first day of school. And the teacher really didn't do much of anything."[1] That this incident occurred in the comfortable Southern California suburb of Cypress led Woods to understand that bigotry and prejudice were not confined to any one part of the country. "People get this stereotype that racism is in the South," he said in an appearance at a Stanford University conference in 1995. "That's B.S. It's everywhere."[2] Woods was still a student and had not yet turned pro, yet he told the same conference of having already received letters telling him "n——s" did not belong in golf. Only nineteen years old, and not yet guarded about avoiding controversy, Tiger also complained about the larger tendency to assume that sports excellence somehow comes easy to black athletes. "We have this stereotype that black players are gifted," Tiger told the Palo Alto crowd, "and white players are heady."[3] He'd already been irritated by coverage that failed to recognize that hard work and willpower were the basis of his own growing success.

Tiger generated controversy of his own by the way he chose to navigate the treacherous waters of American race politics. While kicking back one day in his Stanford dorm room, he coined the neologism "Cablinasian" to describe his mixed heritage — white, black, and Native American through Earl, and Asian from Kultida (who was part Dutch as well as Chinese and Thai herself). The number of interracial marriages in America had doubled between 1980 and 2008, reaching almost 15 percent; increasingly, the children of these mixed unions were identifying as "multiracial," as opposed to "white," "black," "Asian," or any other single category. That Tiger decided to call himself "Cablinasian" made him part of the growing late-twentieth-century embrace of multiracialism.

But multiracialism is still a minority position in the wider sweep of American racial politics. To claim mixed ancestry, after all, runs against the traditional and still very powerful calculus of the so-called one drop of blood rule, or ODR, as scholars abbreviate it. This unspoken yet powerful custom forces you to identify as either "black" or "white," and slots you as black if you have any African ancestry at all. In the age of slavery, the ODR served plantation masters by categorizing their mulatto children by slave women as "black" and thus also enslavable, but it has long since taken on a life of its own. Some civil-rights activists opposed adding a "multiracial" check box to the 2000 census, for fear that any departure from the conventions of the ODR would undercut black numbers, solidarity, and power. One line of thinking portrays "multiracial" as just the latest attempt by people of color to "pass" instead of being proud to be black and united in the face of racism's enduring American reality.

Tiger, the self-proclaimed Cablinasian, became a lightning rod in the debate about multiracialism. The writer Danzy Senna unkindly offered her own satirical definition of Tiger's multiracial moniker: "A rare exotic breed found mostly in California. This is the mother of all mixtures, and when caught may be displayed for large sums of money. . . . A show mulatto, with great performance skills, the Cablinasian will be whoever the crowd wants him to be, and can switch at the drop of a dime. Does not, however, answer to 'black.'"[4] The comedian Dave Chappelle poked fun at Tiger in his wildly popular "Racial Draft" skit. Chappelle played Tiger as a nerd in a racial identity crisis, mumbling to himself about being "so confused, Cablicalasian and so many things." Chappelle's Tiger is delighted to be chosen by "the blacks" in this parody of a professional sports draft, giving him "a race at last." "Good-bye fried rice," he grins, "hello fried chicken!"[5] Some African Americans had been disappointed, in fact, when Tiger first let it be known that he called himself "Cablinasian" in an appearance on the *Oprah Winfrey Show* just after his first Masters triumph. The term's contrivedness made it an easy target for derision, but the discontent was driven by the feeling that Tiger, if not a race traitor, was naïve about racial realities. Even the former secretary of state Colin Powell rebuked the young star: "In America, when you look like me, you're black."

Woods saw it otherwise. Like most others who identified themselves as multiracial, he did not view the Cablinasian label as denying his blackness. Among other things, Tiger did see himself as a black man, and, in fact, spoke of his Masters victory as a "vindication for all the great African American players who never got to play there."[6] Woods was careful to pay tribute to the black golf pioneers in public comments, and Charlie Sifford, the Jackie Robinson of golf, called him "his grandson." But neither did Woods, in his term, want to be "pigeonholed" into any single category. In the Oprah Winfrey interview, the young Tiger explained his reasoning.[7] When faced with the check boxes on "those little forms and stuff," he wasn't able to choose just one: "I usually pick African-American-Asian, because those are the two households I was raised under." To check "black" alone would be to "deny my mom's heritage," Tiger added, while checking only "Asian" would be to "deny my father's heritage. Those are the two I was raised under and those are the only two things I know." By contrast to the zero-sum mathematics of the ODR, where you are either "black" or "white," multiracialism operates by an additive vision of race where you can be more than one thing at a time without being disloyal to any part of your identity. The Cablinasian Tiger was the first African American golfer and also the first Asian American golfer to become the world's top player if one fully accepts this logic (and, in fact, Woods probably has more Asian ancestry than any other, given his father's mixed genealogy).

It's interesting to contrast Tiger and Barack Obama in this light. As similar as the two men's trajectory in other ways, they diverge on the matter of self-identification. Obama adheres to the traditional ODR taxonomy: he calls himself black, albeit in somewhat oxymoronic terms a "black man of mixed heritage." This may be, among other things, a political necessity. It's tricky enough to win high office with a name like Barack Hussein Obama without further complicating matters by adopting the more unconventional argot of multiracialism (and Obama might have alienated, for example, at least some potential black voters had he claimed to be a hybrid, rather than embrace blackness as his principal identity). Although Obama has friends of all colors and speaks proudly of his white mother and grandparents, his personal life bespeaks a desire to consolidate his blackness: wedding a black woman; becoming an activist in inner-city Chicago; joining a black church. Tiger's rainbow inner circle of family and friends included black superstars like Michael Jordan and Charles Barkley. Unlike Obama, however, Woods married white, and belonged to no black institutions, nor did he identify with black political causes. His main man on the golf course, the caddie Steve Williams, was a white New Zealander. The superstar golfer was altogether uninterested in playing by the rules of the one-drop-of-blood system.

But the topic of Tiger's racial affiliation receded and almost vanished with the passing years. A famous Nike ad, "Hello World," had introduced the company's newest pitchman as he turned pro, in 1996; it positioned Tiger as a racial pioneer, quoting him as saying that "there are still some golf courses in the United States that I cannot play because of the color of my skin."[8] This was a one-time only event. Tiger would go on to make hundreds of other commercials without ever again pushing the hot button of race. His public pronouncements focused on the state of his golf game, and his default guardedness extended to avoiding comment about race relations (including anything further about his own heritage beyond Oprah and a Barbara Walters special). Tiger apparently realized early on that race was a no-win game for him. When he'd tried to explain his Cablinasian identity, he'd been the laughing stock of late-night comedy, not to mention being reproved by a former secretary of state and other prominent blacks. And then there had been the trouble with Fuzzy Zoeller at the 1997 Masters. Traditionally, the Masters winner picks the menu for the annual pre-tournament dinner for past champions. As the young Woods pulled away from the field, Zoeller, a former champion, jokingly instructed reporters to tell "the little kid [Woods] . . . not to serve fried chicken or collard greens or whatever the hell they serve." The comments caused a small uproar, and K-Mart, Zoeller's main sponsor, severed its ties with the veteran pro. But Tiger was also criticized. Several pros felt, as one put it, that Woods had left Zoeller "out to dry" by not immediately coming forward to forgive him and make things right. This was puzzling logic, since it was Zoeller's stupid, borderline racist joke that had caused the trouble in the first place (and some observers suspected that the real reason other pros were critical of Tiger had to do with jealousy at the fuss being made over the new superstar). In any event, Tiger had been derided when he opened up about his own racial identity, yet now, when he remained silent, found himself criticized just the same. It's perhaps not so surprising that Tiger would choose to avoid race altogether since it only seemed to cause unintended trouble for a man who disliked distractions in the first place.

Increasingly, too, Tiger transcended race altogether, or so it sometimes seemed in his early-twenty-first-century glory years. Earl and Kultida had named their only child Eldrick Tont Wood (they used the first letters of their own names for the first and last letter of his first name to signify their bookend love for the baby). The nickname "Tiger" came from a South Vietnamese army officer who had once saved Earl's life in Vietnam and died in a North Vietnamese prison camp. As the young man's fame grew, he was no longer Eldrick Woods, the stuttering elementary-schooler with thick nerdy black glasses. He became Tiger Woods, and then just Tiger, the superstar, the brand, the golf god. Does Zeus have a race? It came to seem inappropriate and almost vulgar to raise the petty matters of racism and skin color in the case of so Olympian an icon as Tiger, especially as he himself never did.

Black criticism of Tiger mostly melted away. Early in his original campaign for the presidency, Barack Obama had also found some black voters to be skeptical of whether he was sufficiently "black," given his white mother and Kenyan father, and ostensible lack of family connection to the African American experience of slavery and Jim Crow. But, among other factors, a developing pride in

Obama's accomplishments eventually led to almost universal black support and acclaim for his election. Similarly, as Tiger's feats became legendary, many black golf fans embraced him as well, the furor over his Cablinasian comments fading into the background (though a few critics now and then surfaced to criticize Woods for not doing enough for blacks in golf).[9] For the first time, black patrons began attending PGA tournaments in sizeable numbers. Virtually all of them followed Tiger.

That Tiger kept quiet about race also matched the mood of America's white majority. Almost half a century after the civil-rights movement, many observers wanted to imagine that the race problem had been "fixed." Don't blacks and other minorities now have equal rights? Or even unfair special advantages as affirmative-action opponents insist? And hasn't America now elected a black man to the presidency? This familiar conservative reasoning fixes just about anyone who persists in talking about racial inequality as a politically correct whiner. Tiger Woods was the perfect hero for a post-racial, post-civil-rights America. He almost never brought up the awkward matters of race and the color line, at least in public, much less point a reproachful finger at whites. To the contrary, the amazing success of this young brown-skinned man in a formerly white sport seemed to support the familiar Fox News, Rush Limbaugh-style view that the only real impediments to black advancement are black laziness, broken families, or, as a more explicitly racist view has it, inferior genes—in other words, that the blame for inner-city violence and persisting poverty lies with blacks alone. When white golf fans cheered for Tiger, it sometimes felt as if they were also congratulating themselves, demonstrating their own enlightened racial good will by embracing a golfer of color. By this way of thinking, those roars for Tiger provided yet more proof that Martin Luther King Jr.'s great dream of a color-blind society was close to realization, if not already realized, at last.

And, of course, America has indeed made great progress since the days of Earl Woods and the legalized apartheid of Jim Crow. Scholars of good faith can disagree about the social and historical reasons that blacks remain poorer than other Americans, and the subject has long been favorite matter for academic debate. But it's beyond question that skin color still structures a great deal of twenty-first-century American life (and it's the great paradox of race that something so utterly trivial as skin pigmentation means so much to us in a supposedly enlightened age). Our society leans to racial endogamy in marriage, friendship, churchgoing, and much else. Despite some new minority prosperity and an increasing divide between those who have entered the middle classes and those left behind, the statistics also show that the average income of black, Latino, and Native American families remains much lower than that of their white counterparts.[10] This means, in turn, that children of color are far more likely to attend substandard schools, grow up in crime-plagued neighborhoods, confront troubled family situations, and other difficulties. We are still far from anything like the post-racial garden of justice and plenty where every child has the same reasonable opportunity for a happy, productive life.

The trajectory of golf says a great deal about race's changing role in national life. Surprisingly, perhaps, the game was an early battleground in the civil-rights movement. By 1955, the U.S. Supreme Court had already handed down *Brown vs. Board of Education*, but protest for racial justice and democracy was only beginning to gather force. A sore spot for golf-loving African Americans, most of whom had learned the game by caddying, was being banned from public-owned municipal courses across the South and parts of the Midwest. George Simkins, a Greensboro dentist who later headed the local NAACP chapter, and five of his friends decided that must change. On a December day in 1955, the Greensboro Six, as they came to be known, walked into the clubhouse at the Gillespie Park public course and each put down their seventy-five cent green fee. Then the men headed to the first tee and, even though an angry

The Greensboro Six (from left to right): Phillip Cook, Sam Murray, Elijah Herring, Joseph Sturdivant, George Simkins, and Leon Wolfe, 1955. Courtesy of *American Golfer*.

club pro at one point tried to get them off the course, finished their round. That night, the police arrested Simkins and his friends for trespassing. The Supreme Court ruled five to four against the golfer-activists, but Gillespie Park was eventually forced to open to all comers (a measure delayed for several years when local whites burned down the clubhouse in spite). Other black golfers, among them crack player Ann Gregory, in her hometown of Gary, Indiana, led similar "play-ins" in those same years.

The Greensboro Six took action five years before the more famous lunch-counter sit-ins and ten years before Martin Luther King Jr.'s march to Selma. It may be that the fight for the right to play golf somehow doesn't sound as inspiring as the struggle for the vote or education, but for whatever reason, the action of Simkins and the others is something of a forgotten episode in civil-rights history (a Duke University history professor and friend of mine who specializes in the movement had not even heard of it until I told him the story). All the same, the Gillespie Park protest was revolutionary action in its own way. This early example of civil disobedience occurred in the very same week that Rosa Parks refused to give up her seat to a white passenger on a Birmingham bus. It underscored the larger dimensions of the civil-rights movement as well. The struggle was about the lofty principles of justice and equality and, at the same time, the black desire for full, credit-card-carrying citizenship in what the historian Lizabeth Cohen calls the "consumer republic."[11] That meant being accorded the same right to shop and spend at department stores, restaurants, hotels, and, yes, golf courses as every other American.

The struggle against discrimination in professional golf was also joined in those years. Joe Louis, the heavyweight champion turned golf aficionado, led the fight. The Brown Bomber became a national hero after his defeat of the Nazi-promoted German Max Schmelling in 1937. Still, some critics have faulted Louis for not speaking out against lynching and the evils of Jim Crow, describing him as having entered into an unspoken "racial bargain" where he won mainstream adulation in exchange for his silence (a charge reminiscent of that leveled by some against Tiger more than a half century later). In fact, after retiring from the ring, Louis did become a fierce critic of America's racial caste system, at least when it came to golf. Although he was not nearly as good at golf as the top black players, Louis wanted to try his hand at professional golf, and was angered by the tour's Caucasians-only clause. He succeeded in shaming tournament officials into allowing him into the San Diego Open in 1952 and thereby became the first black player ever to compete in a PGA tournament. He then got both himself and three of the other best black players, including Charles Sifford, an invitation to the Phoenix Open several weeks later. On the first hole, Louis and his companions found that the cup had been packed with human feces. He and the others continued the round undeterred. The former boxing champion, pulling no punches now, called the PGA president Horton Smith "an American Hitler" and went on the attack to demand the abolition of the Caucasians-only clause. It was in large measure thanks to Louis's intervention that the clause was at last repealed in 1961.

It might appear that golf no longer has a race problem. If you watch tournaments on television, you've probably seen those kumbaya-like ads, of smiling minority kids with golf clubs, for First Tee, a program that encourages underprivileged children to take up the game. That the game's most famous superstar, Tiger Woods, is now a man of color would seem to be the ultimate confirmation of the sport having moved beyond its racist past. But, in fact, professional golf has regressed in terms of diversity and inclusiveness, at least with regard to African Americans. In the 1970s, eleven black pros played the PGA tour; they included stars like Sifford, Lee Elder (the first black man invited to the Masters), Jim Dent, and Calvin Peete. Peete, the first and only PGA tour player with diamonds inlaid in his front teeth, had labored as a migrant farmworker to support his family until making it pro in his twenties. He was a short, slender man with a crooked left arm, from a childhood injury that had never healed properly, and yet he was one of the most accurate, consistent players of his day and won the prestigious Players Championship in 1985. By contrast, Tiger has for most of his career been the only African American, if one counts him as that, on the 125-member PGA tour circuit.[12] Not one black player is on the Nationwide, the golf equivalent of the minor leagues, and there are none in any major college program, the traditional feeders of professional golf. No African American has played on the women's professional tour, the LPGA, for more than three decades.

Several factors explain the dearth of black professionals. Technology is one culprit, in particular the golf cart. Caddying has long been a back door into golf for the poor and disadvantaged. Like Walter Hagen and Gene Sarazen, several legendary champions from humble backgrounds got their start carrying bags at country clubs. Except for Calvin Peete, all the black professionals of the 1960s and 1970s learned the game caddying. But the invention of the motorized golf cart reduced the use of caddies to only the fanciest courses, and in the process closed that doorway into golf. At the same time, the game's globalization has raised the skill level demanded to compete professionally. As golf has grown in Asia, Europe, and other regions, those areas have begun to produce more world-class players. International golfers now hold twenty-nine of the top fifty spots in the men's world ranking, including stars from Australia, Argentina, Northern Ireland, Taiwan, and Spain. There are only ten Americans in the women's top fifty (and in a sign of the trivializing sexism with which women must too often still contend, a Google search for "female top fifty golfers" pulls up "top fifty hottest female golfers of all time" as the first result). This means that a young black golfer must now compete with a vastly expanded pool of players that includes dozens of first-rate international golfers for a coveted PGA tour spot (this remains the most prestigious circuit, even with the establishment of major professional tours in Europe and Asia).

Money remains perhaps the biggest obstacle to minority golf advancement. The performance standard has been raised in every professional sport with advanced training methods, nutrition, video instruction, and other tools. Golf is no exception. It's very difficult to take up the game in adolescence or young adulthood and become a world-class golfer, as men like Calvin Peete, Lee Trevino, and Larry Nelson did in an older day. Earl Woods established the new paradigm for golf training by getting a golf club into Tiger's hands even before he could walk. But giving a child an early start is pricey, with money required for equipment, instruction, membership at a course with top-class facilities, travel to junior tournaments, and tuition at a golf-training academy. That America's structures of race and class still overlap means that black families find themselves far less likely than white ones to have the money it takes to raise a top golfer (and, of course, children in many inner-city neighborhoods do not have access to golf courses of any kind). The money handicap helps to explain the dearth of American-born Latino and Native American pros as well as of white ones from working-class origins. An increasing number of Asian American families do have the necessary resources, and, not coincidentally, Asian Americans are the single minority group with a growing representation on both the men's and women's professional tours. It would take a massive investment of resources by the tour to increase the numbers of black and Latino golfers (and much more than the First Tee program, which has not yet produced a single touring pro).

But the golf establishment tilts to the Right politically, including the professional tour. Many players come from affluent, Southern, evangelical backgrounds, and one recent survey showed that only two of the 125 PGA touring pros are Democrats; nine of them oppose abortion rights and gun control; and four out of five supported the invasion of Iraq. The likes of Rush Limbaugh and Dan Quayle make frequent appearances at pro-am tournaments (the former vice president's wife once famously reported that "Dan would rather play golf than have sex any time"). The climate, in short, does not lend itself to any particular concern for diversity, much less to the sort of sustained effort to look more like America that the NBA, NFL, and even Major League Baseball have made with regard to coaching and front-office positions. Even the traditional Southern white sport of NASCAR has done better than golf, with a well-funded "Drive to Diversity" program (and such initiatives can also be good for business insofar as showcasing athletes of more varied backgrounds can expand a sport's fan base).

The lack of black pros sheds light on the broader dynamics of racial inequality in America now. As evidenced in the hate-mail

Tiger received when he joined the tour, the old problems of bigotry, hatred, and discrimination, both direct and subtle, have not disappeared. But now that it's illegal to discriminate and the vast majority of Americans believe at least in principle in racial equality, the explanation for persisting racial barriers tends to involve a constellation of overlapping, sometimes hidden factors: technology, globalization, economic inequalities, and the lack of proactive effort to integrate in the case of professional golf. Because addressing racial issues is no longer a simple matter of repealing discriminatory laws or any other single magic bullet, the challenge of change in golf and society itself is all the harder. Progress demands the patient, multilevel coordination and commitment that has been lacking in professional golf. Some golf defenders will reply that whites are underrepresented in the NBA and NFL, yet no one complains about this. But any kid good enough to play in the NBA and NFL can do so, these leagues being genuine meritocracies. By contrast, most poor minority kids simply never have the chance to become professional golfers due to their economic circumstances. Having more African American sports professionals may not top the list of urgent social problems demanding remedy. Even so, there'd surely be more great black and Latino players if the playing field were level. That there are so few indexes the inequality of opportunity that still defines the graphs of race, success, and privilege in this country.

I should add that race continues to figure into golf at many other levels. Golf equipment is a multibillion dollar industry, between the balls, clubs, gloves, clothes, training aids, and dozens of other gizmos. And yet, the gigantic annual equipment trade show in Orlando could be mistaken for some sort of white people's convention, given its lack of minorities among both executives and sales forces. The big companies, like Callaway and Taylormade, outsource their club manufacturing to factories staffed by low-paid female workers in China and, more recently, in Vietnam and Cambodia. The industry, in other words, operates by a hierarchy of race and gender com-

Female worker at a golf-club manufacturing plant in China, 2007. Courtesy of *Golf Digest*. Photo by J. D. Cuban.

manded by affluent white executives, with poor Asian women doing the heavy labor for a few dollars a day. The numbers of black weekend players have grown considerably in recent years, and African Americans now make up roughly two million of America's twenty-five million recreational golfers (one of the fastest growing golf demographics is black women). But most exclusive clubs and top courses also remain overwhelmingly white, many with no black or even Asian members at all.

And consider who does the upkeep grunt work at golf courses. We have an image of the archetypal golf maintenance man as a working-class white guy in the model of Bill Murray's grubby, obsessed stoner, Carl Spackler, in the classic comedy *Caddyshack* (which Tiger cites as his favorite golf movie). Golf has instead be-

Latino maintenance man at a Palm Springs, California, golf course, 2008.
Photo by Orin Starn.

come a new kind of migrant farm labor. Latin American immigrants do much of grass-cutting, weed-whacking, and other dirty work. These men, who seldom earn much more than minimum wage, arrive for work in the predawn dark in order to be out of the way by the time the first golfers tee off. That most golfers do not see the labor that goes into keeping up a course is an example of what the geographer Stephen Daniels has called the "duplicity of landscape."[13] Here again golf presents a juxtaposition between wealthy white men and poor brown-skinned laborers in an arrangement that, like too much else in twenty-first-century America, does not look postracial at all.

It would be nice to imagine that those Latino maintenance men, not to mention the Chinese golf-club factory workers, might someday receive cosmic compensation for their labors. Early one morning at South Carolina's Big Blue Golf Club, I chatted with a young Guatemalan man named Juan, who was raking a last sand trap before leaving for the day. I asked if he played golf, and he said only soccer, but that he had a baby son back home in the village. This was before Tigergate, and Tiger was still the gold standard for sporting success and glory. "*Pues*," Juan said, "maybe he'll be the next Tiger Woods and I'll never have to work again." He smiled as if perfectly aware of the improbability of any such fairytale ending.

6

TIGER'S PENIS

A memorable scene from Spike Lee's *Do The Right Thing* features Mookie, the pizza delivery man, questioning Pino, the pizzeria's owner's son, about his rage against black people. It turns out that Pino's favorite basketball player, movie actor, and rock star are Magic Johnson, Eddie Murphy, and Prince, respectively. Mookie, played by Lee himself, notes the obvious contradiction: "Pino, all you ever say is 'n-this and 'n-that," and all your favorite people are so-called n——s." Pino struggles to explain: "Magic, Eddie, Prince, they're not n——s. I mean, they're not black. I mean . . . let me explain myself. . . ." Here Lee captures how celebrity can endow African Americans with a partial exemption from the racial hatred and stereotyping faced by more everyday people, all the way back to Sammy Davis Jr. and Willie Mays and up to Denzel Washington and other more modern luminaries.

Tiger lost that free pass in the infidelity scandal. Mainstream media outlets steered clear of bringing race into Tigergate, but not the blogs, message boards, and forums. The disjunction between public and private in race talk is typical of America today. A recently landed space alien might think that we were a completely enlightened, racism-free country, to judge by the airwaves, the newspapers, and the political speeches. Only the very stupid haters now and then voice anything like racist opinions on the record. By contrast, the Internet's anonymity allows for the circulation of racial jokes, hatred, and stereotyping of every stripe. In an earlier day, as the anthropologist John Jackson argues, racism remained "explicit, obvious, and legal"; usually, "what blacks saw was what they got." But what now prevails is a "racial paranoia" characterized by "extremist thinking, general social distrust, the nonfalsifiable embrace of intuition, and an unflinching commitment to contradictory thinking."[1] Rumors about whites blowing up the levees to flood black New Orleans neighborhoods and other such conspiracy theories are more extreme versions of this distrust, but it extends to more subtle, everyday worries. Take, for example, a black shopper wondering if a salesperson is dawdling in serving her because of some racist animus, or a Latino college student fearing classmates may think he only got in through affirmative action. Whites have our own varied forms of racial paranoia. There's the proverbial suspicious woman clutching a purse by habit whenever she sees a young black man in an elevator, or the would-be good white liberal who fears letting slip some racial epithet in mixed company. Along with the birther theory, the more conservative brands of white racial fear include the conviction that Barack Obama is a Muslim or that he harbors a "deep-seated hatred for white people" (as the Fox News commentator Glenn Beck once asserted). The sway of political correctness and accompanying fear of getting into trouble mean that racial anxiety and distrust often find most direct expression in the surreptitious, off-stage arenas of our private thoughts, a talk with a friend or, most accessible to the anthropologist, an anonymous post on some blog, comment board, or chat room.

Indeed, the extent of Tiger's fall from grace—in particular, the expiration of his exemption from racist hatred and stereotyping—was on full display in the backchannels of the Web. What one finds posted on the Internet, of course, never neatly mirrors society; it's often those with particular axes to grind and plenty of time on their hands who log on to have their say (and not to mention those "trollers" who put up nasty comments just to see the reaction). But the ugly racial commentary around Tigergate was too voluminous to be written off as the ranting of a few cranks or haters. If surely not representative of the American majorities, the thousands of racially-charged, sometimes outright racist posts pointed to persisting and still quite powerful riptides of prejudice and worse. The alchemy of Internet anonymity and strong opinion about Tiger's troubles drove America's dark racial id up into the viewable pixilated channels of the chatrooms, e-mail lists and other public realms of cyberspace.

Consider a doctored picture of Woods with Snoop Dogg that circulated not long after the scandal broke. A friend forwarded it to me; he had received it through an e-mail tree, with the owner unidentified so as to protect the sender from any repercussions (the picture itself also bears no credit, its creator perhaps also fearful about potential trouble for playing around with the explosive matter of race). The picture inverts the standard personae of the two stars: Snoop, who actually does play golf, appears in preppy, country-club garb; Tiger wears the jaunty porkpie hat, silver chain, and fur coat of the stereotypical black "player" with a stable of women and appetite for sex and money. The caption reads "PIMPIN' There's no b'ness like hoe b'ness," and both men smile broadly, as if well-pleased with themselves. This particular exercise in politically incorrect guerrilla cybercaricature pulled Tiger off his pedestal as the megacelebrity above the racial fray. Here the great golfer is no longer Tiger, the

Anonymously doctored photo depicting Tiger and Snoop Dogg in inverted roles, 2010.

postracial icon. The anonymous graphic artist recasts Woods, as Pino would doubtless have it, as just another n——, albeit perhaps an enviable one in that peculiar popular-culture turn that has made pimping into something positive in more recent parlance.

The literary theorist Maurice Wallace notes how black men have often been confined to a repertoire of limited, rigid, and dichotomous images.[2] In slave times, we had the "good n——" and the "bad n——"; in the more modern updating, we have the unthreatening, Clifford Huxtable-style black suburban professional and his dangerous inverse, the tough, hypermacho inner-city gangsta. In the latter way of seeing, according to Michael Kimmel, young black men "are all violence, athletics prowess, aggression, and sexual predation."[3] This persona provokes fear, anxiety, and contempt—yet also a kind of envy and vicarious identification helps to explain the vast popularity of hip-hop and hood style among white suburban youth. The gangsta is a latter-day version of those two older iconic boyhood-fantasy figures, the pirate and the Indian warrior, in signifying the freedom and the power to do what you want and not, as 2Pac brags, "give a fuck" about the consequences.

That Tigergate had activated the stereotype of hypersexualized black masculinity in its crudest, most hateful forms was evident enough in Internet postings. "So typical of a nig*r," as GoBacktotheWoods proclaimed on the website Hollywood Gossip with unembarrassed racist spite. "Can't wait to be with a white slut, or in this case of a black chink, a whole lot of 'em. . . . Of course, the only way a white whore (including his wife) would be with this bug-eyed brillo head, bucktoothed spook is for money (that's what prostitutes do)." FookMi tied Tiger's sexual appetite for white women to the old racist trope of the dumb, lazy n———: "All this fucking knuckle dragger needs is a bucket of chicken, a watermelon, and a Hi-C to heaven here on earth." It was impossible to say whether they were white, black, Latino, or what, but some posters cheered Tiger's extracurricular activities in that macho spirit of admiration for the "player" and gangsta-style predatory sexuality. Marshmallow's long post on Hollywood Gossip put a new spin on the iconography of Tiger Woods as a latter-day divinity. Tiger, Marshmallow wrote, "should be worshipped like God in human form. He has banged more women than the average fully grown rapper. If ya know what I'm sayin."

Of course, the celebration of gangsta sexual prowess very often has misogyny for a twin traveler. Countless Internet posters variously derided Tiger's mistresses as "h———s," "trash," "nasty females," or, in the case of Smooth, another admirer in the style of Marshmallow, "b———es": "Tiger's wife is plain and boring. This kinky dude needed to get some wild tail. Do what you gotta do Tiger. Just pay those B*X$%@S off and get otta there my Brother." Only a few posters questioned the entire assumption of black male hypersexuality and unfaithfulness. "President Obama didn't cheat," NIG added to the Hollywood Gossip thread. "Michael Jordan didn't cheat [although, in that case, Jordan himself admitted after his divorce that he had]. J. Lo's husband didn't cheat. Linkin Park's lead singer didn't cheat, my Dad didn't cheat."

A stock flashpoint for fear and fantasy about black masculinity is, of course, penis size. As the cultural critic Scott Poulson-Bryant notes in his provocative *Hung: A Meditation on the Measure of Black Men in America*, black men have long been "hung" on the image of "the sexual beast, the loin-engaged predator, the big-dicked destroyer."[4] Paulson-Bryant means us to see this "hanging" in a double sense: literally, as in the early-twentieth-century lynching of black men accused of "despoiling" white women, and culturally, as a stereotype that black men have to deal with even today. In a bawdy profile of the golfer John Daly, the sportswriter Rick Reilly relates that Daly got the nickname "Long John" not just for his titanic drives, but also from possessing a "flabbergastingly large" penis, like a "Hebrew National or perhaps the leg of a very large beechwood credenza."[5] Even so, one doesn't normally read speculation about how big the genitals of white celebrities and athletes may be. For example, Internet posters did not spend time discussing the penis of Ben Roethlisberger, the white Pittsburgh Steelers quarterback who was caught in his own sex scandal, following his alleged rape of a college student and other incidents. That Tiger was black, or at least Cablinasian, made his case different, and his penis size into an instant object of curiosity. A few months into Tigergate, "Tiger Woods penis" already produced more than 130,00 Google hits. A rumor circulated that *Playgirl* was going to publish pictures of Tiger's genitalia. The first question for Joslyn James, Wood's porn-star liaison, during a *Playboy* radio talk show was, yes, about how "big Tiger is." Far from being limited to trash media, the frenzy around Tiger's member extended into more literate, liberal, would-be enlightened fora. The *Huffington Post* ran a tasteless spoof news release by the satirist Andy Borowitz, a frequent *New Yorker* contributor, under the title "Tiger's Penis Signs Seven-Figure Book Deal."[6] And several porn sites montaged pictures of a smiling Tiger in golf garb next to explicit close-ups of a white woman having sex with a black man with a large penis, as if to suggest that the man was Woods. As several critics have observed, white men seem to like black-male-with-white female pornography and its titillation at taboo-breaking, a predilection in line with the odd, contradictory mix of loathing, envy, and fantasy surrounding black male sexuality (and white female sexuality, too, in a different way).[7] Once the outsized action hero of the golf world, Tiger was cut down to a single body part by this coarse modern variant of the primordial racist trope of black savagery: the big black phallus.

Ironically, Tiger, the Cablinasian, did not see himself through the same lens. He was not one of those stereotypical woman-attracting, big-dicked black men in his own eyes, or at least not sure he was. The journalist Charles Pierce, who profiled Tiger for GQ in 1997, accompanied the then twenty-year-old superstar on the limousine ride to a magazine cover shoot. Along the way, Tiger addressed the driver, a black former Vanderbilt University basketball player: "What I can't figure out is why so many good-looking women hang around baseball and basketball. Is it because, you know, people always say that, like, black guys have big dicks?" At the studio, Tiger told various dirty jokes, one returning to the theme of big black phallus. "What's this?," he asked the flirty young women who were attending to his wardrobe, rubbing his shoe tips against each other: "It's a black guy taking off his condom." The punch line of Woods's subsequent Little Rascal joke had Buckwheat performing fellatio on his white teacher, and he followed that up with a lesbian joke: "Why do two lesbians arrive faster than two gay guys? Because they're always doing 69."[8] The article's publication led to some censure of Tiger, but the glow around the young man Oprah had just labeled as "America's son" was so great that his jokes were mostly excused as just the typical tasteless kegger humor of someone his age. That Pierce reported Tiger's offstage banter and joking would later be cited one reason that Woods grew so guarded with journalists.

In the story, Tiger came across as ambivalent about his own racial identity. One might take the condom joke for a boast: a black man reveling in his own supposed phallic superiority. Yet the comment to the limo driver—and that Woods told his whole series of jokes in the style of a man making fun of other groups (gays, lesbians, African Americans)—suggests that he did not completely or even at all identify himself as the proverbial potent black man. In his "sexts" to Joslyn James more than decade later, Tiger sounded more than anything like the nerdy white guy of Chappelle's impersonation, fantasizing about "wearing out" the porn star ("I would love to have the ability to make you sore").[9] When Jaimee Grubbs, another mistress, told Tiger that golf bored her and that she only watched football, he replied: "Figured you would say that. Big black guys." Once again, Woods appeared to be positioning himself as something other than or at least not quite the same as the virile black man. Later in the thread with Grubbs, in fact, he referenced his own mixed identity. "Having an asian mother and a military father," he wrote, means "you cannot and will not ever be full of yourself." When Grubbs texted about falling "more and more for u," Tiger attributed that to his ancestry: "Because I'm blasian ☺," he answered.[10] Here Woods was reworking the more common equation of black masculinity with romantic conquest to claim his hybridity as the basis of his attraction (even if other messages suggests he knew that money and fame were his biggest aphrodisiacs). All of us live our fantasy and real lives within a topography of the imagination characterized by powerful old stereotypes about race, gender, and sexuality. At the same time, many, perhaps all, Americans of every hue feel that these stupid, banal, and often racist and sexist forms of classification and imagination do not do justice to our own individuality. Woods was very much the same way. He was taken in and perhaps partly identified with the myth of the hung black man, and yet also kept his distance from it as Tida and Earl's dutiful Cablinasian son.

Some African Americans viewed the uproar over Tigergate as just more evidence of white racism. "Leave the man alone," posted spiritualman56 on the ABC News/Entertainment website, then blamed "BOSS MEDIA" for using any "black person they can get to fill their bank account" and then stabbing him in the back. Fedup advanced the same argument on Bossip, the self-proclaimed "premier website for African-American and Black celebrity gossip": "The media having a field day to see a black man with all this money is falling **down** the tubes. The white man lives to see that!" This way of thinking portrayed Tigergate as little more than another case of The Man tearing down successful people of color. It was impossible to prove or disprove this sweeping claim any more than the other forms of "racial paranoia" that John Jackson attributes to the post-civil-rights, "affirmative action baby" generation (and he does not mean to suggest whether such paranoia is justifiable or not, only that it figures powerfully in twenty-first-century racial imagination).

Another consequence of Tigergate was to reopen debate among African Americans about whether Woods was really one of them. Although Tiger's marriage to Elin had provoked some backlash from black women upset that he had chosen a white woman, the talk about whether he was "black enough" had died down in more recent years. The rapper Nas had even given a shout out to Tiger for "reppin' us hard" along with an eclectic list of other black luminaries including the retired NFL star Jim Brown, civil-rights activist Stokely Carmichael, poet Nikki Giovanni, and murdered Nigerian music legend Fela. But Tigergate resurrected older doubts about Woods's racial allegiances, and generated new accusations that he was an outright race traitor. In a YouTube clip, for example, a younger black man calling himself DiscoSean21 said he'd been sent an open letter to Woods, and he read it to the camera: "Dear Tiger Woods, We stood behind Kobe Bryant when he cheated on his wife. We also supported

O. J. Simpson when they said he took another life. We also backed Michael Jackson when he was accused of touching a little boy. But since you don't claim to be one of us, you've got to face this on your own. Sincerely yours, The N——s."[11]

This calculus of racial authenticity made declared allegiance to blackness into the ultimate litmus test. Kobe Bryant was raised in Italy and the Philadelphia Main Line in plush family circumstances; O. J. Simpson, another golf nut, had been a version of the corporate-friendly, unthreatening black man; and Jackson had sought to whiten his features in countless plastic surgeries. None of these men had gone so far as to claim to be anything other than black, however, and they therefore enjoyed the support of the self-proclaimed "N-s." Predictably, one poster took offense that the letter seemed to suggest that because "some one is some race" they should be "exept" (*sic*) from criticism. The "N——s" who sent the missive were just "more punkass internet gangstas," in plutoisacommet's more sanguine opinion. The feeling that Tigergate was just comeuppance for Tiger's refusal to identify as black was nonetheless common in black-frequented circuits of cyberworld. "I must say," posted Fedup on Bossip, "I was done with his sorry behind the minute he said he was 'Casublisian.'"

Tiger's apparent preference for white women only confirmed his betrayal of his blackness for Fedup and others. "Guess no 'chocolate' ladies need apply," observed Mr. Obvious on Hollywood Gossip. "WHITE WOMEN ONLY. Tiger Woods is a RACIST!," added Steve. "He will tap a white trash pancake house waitress but will not dip the wick into a black she-boon." To accompany a report on Tiger's troubles, *Vanity Fair* featured a cover photo of the golfer shirtless in a bad-boy hip-hop pose. This previously unpublished shot, taken in 2006 by the famous photographer Annie Leibovitz, "blackened" Woods, both literally, in its dark tones, and figuratively, in promoting his improbable new image as some sort of gangsterish inner-city hood. By contrast, and far from "darkening" Tiger, the

Vanity Fair cover, by Annie Leibovitz, 2010.

scandal had "lightened" him in the eyes of Steve and Mr. Obvious. Some people, black and white, had viewed Woods as white all along, a golf nerd and not a bad boy, the proverbial "Oreo." Now one black blogger even declared Tiger to be "Black Enemy Number One."[12] This was a far cry from the likes of spiritualman56 and others who defended Woods as another black victim of the white media.

These varied opinions underscore the decidedly plural, sometimes directly opposed ways in which Americans even of supposedly similar racial backgrounds make sense of race politics. It was an interesting twist to find at least some black posters applying the word *racist* to Tiger. The civil-rights movement first brought *racism* into widespread American use in the 1950s and 1960s, its original incarnation serving as shorthand for Jim Crow and hatred against blacks. The rapper Griff, of Public Enemy, would later seek to restrict broader usage by insisting that only whites could be racists. Spike Lee, who used Public Enemy's "Fight the Power" in the soundtrack for *Do the Right Thing*, sought to justify that logic: "Black folks can't be racist. White folks invented that shit!"[13] According to this definition, racism was not simply hatred and prejudice, but institutionalized bigotry, and thus could only be practiced by those in power. But, in more recent years, conservatives have sought to recode the term, and to turn it back against blacks it perceives to be antiwhite. Thus, for example, the websites of right-wing groups like Confederate States of America decry the latest examples of reverse racism; the former Republican house speaker Newt Gingrich opposed the Supreme Court Justice nominee Sonia Sotomayor for supposedly being "a racist"; and, in the middle of Tigergate, Fox News tried to get an African American official in the Department of Agriculture fired for "racist comments" before the NAACP (and in that case had to issue an apology when the official turned out to have been quoted grossly out of context, from a speech that actually endorsed colorblind assistance to poor farmers). Like most brands of racial paranoia, the new white obsession with "reverse racism" has just enough truth to it to make it credible to the predisposed. A college applicant with poor white parents may indeed not get the same bump as one with rich black ones in our current system, which favors race over class in affirmative action (and you could just as well argue that both forms of assistance remain justified for the time being to remedy patterns of exclusion in higher education and elsewhere). The debate about racism has so shifted that the NAACP, which once denounced racism only against people of color, recently went on record that its "zero tolerance policy" applies whether racial discrimination is "practiced by blacks, whites, or any other group."[14] That the Cablinasian Tiger would find himself denounced as a "racist" in so many posts evinced how the term has become unmoored enough from its original American connotation to be applied now to hatred no matter the color of the skin.

Tiger's apparent preference for white women especially infuriated some black women.[15] Although the idea that blacks should not marry "outside the race" has a long history, with advocates as diverse as Marcus Garvey, Booker T. Washington, and Malcolm X, the feelings of more modern-day black women have also to do with the changing sociology of race and love. Interracial unions have become more common in recent decades, but not across the board. In 2008, a study found that 22 percent of black men wedded nonblack women; only 9 percent of black women married nonblack men.[16] Among other explanations for these figures are the tiresome orthodox standards of feminine beauty and attraction, which still tend to value whiteness over blackness in twenty-first century America, giving white women that advantage. Conversely, the properties of coolness, potency, and virility attached to the stereotypical black manhood can endow it with a certain cachet in these new times. In antebellum days, the union of white men and black women was the predominant form of cross-racial sexual contact, whether in Jefferson- and Hemmings-style concubinage or in the outright rape of slave women by slave masters. Almost two centuries later, it's the other way around, at least judging by the marriage rates. It has become harder for black women to find marriageable men, in particular black men, with more than a million of them behind bars or killed in street violence. All this figures into the currents of cynicism and sometimes outrage among a certain number of black women about both black men who marry white and the white women who seem to be stealing "their" men (various Internet posters described Elin as a "gold-digger" and "nanyy [sic] who hit the jackpot"; Tiger's mistresses figured as "nasty females" and "run-through, collagen-lipped, tattle-telling models, waitresses, hostesses, or **** stars").

You could see the ire in the running commentary about Tiger. The negative views about his original union with Elin were relatively kind compared to the vitriol about his extramarital affairs. Antigerb63 suggested that Tiger was not only a "a big time racist doing high order racial discrimination against black women," but also that he "should be beaten by a dozen strong black women, plus his wife." If the likes of Steve and Mr. Obvious saw Tiger's racial tastes as evidence the golfer was somehow not black enough, a healthy subset of black women posters took the opposite view, that he was altogether too black, and in particular too much like the stereotypical black man. Dave Chappelle had cleverly captured the idea of an affinity for white women as a black male trait in his "Racial Draft" skit, before Tiger and Elin had married. When the "black delegation" picks Woods for their racial team in the comedian's satire of ESPN-style professional sports drafts and American racial politics, the Asians in the crowd boo and look disappointed. But the black announcer says it makes sense: "He's been discriminated against in his time; he's had death threats; and he dates a white woman. Sounds like a black guy to me." A feeling of betrayal led some black women to urge others to their own racial crossing following Tigergate. Smartandsexy offered the following advice on the Hip-Hop Wired website (and also demonstrated the now common homophobic redefinition of *gay* as a synonym for *rotten* or *messed up*): "BLACK

MEN ARE GAY. DOPE HEADS, JAIL BIRDS, OR JUST PLAIN SORRY. BLACK WOMEN GET A WHITE MAN, OPEN YOUR EYES . . . WHITE MEN HAVE MONEY, POWER, SMOOTH TANNED SKIN AND ARE GORGEOUS. THIS IS COMING FROM AN ENLIGHTENED BLACK WOMAN! WAKE UP SISTAS!!!!!!!" The American racial labyrinth has long led to strange, seemingly unlikely convergences on certain points. Thus, for example, an outspoken black nationalist like Marcus Garvey and Jim Crow white supremacists could agree that blacks and whites would be better off apart from one another. In this more modern case, the venting of angry African American women like Smartandsexy sounded much like the negative, racist stereotyping of black men you'd expect to hear from some Aryan nation follower, Tigergate being the precipitating cause of their displeasure.

Many Americans, mostly white, have grown cynical and even resentful about race talk of any kind. These sentiments underlay the objections from some message board pundits to any claim that race had any part whatsoever in Tiger's behavior or the Tigergate coverage. An outraged Brittany posted on Hollywood Gossip: "Im sick and tired of hearing this thing get turned around into some racial bullshit. . . . Tiger is just a man whore. It just happens to be that none of them were colored. Enough is Enough. Colored ppl are the ones who are still keeping racism around." "Look at all the ignorant human debris on here talking about race," added Me on the black-oriented Hip-Hop Wired. "Go figure. I HATE black **people** who always act like white **people** hold them **down** and act like the world needs to just hand them shit. Get a job, or kill yourself. Please?" The concept of racism as an obstacle to achievement has always coexisted uneasily with the archetypal American ideals of self-help and individual responsibility. The comments from Brittany and Me measure a view that any African American invocation of racism is merely an exercise in victimology and excuse-making. Although it's mostly whites who take such cynical position (and also a fair number of Latinos and Asians), a tradition of demanding self-reliance also runs through the black activist tradition. Booker T. Washington was famously acerbic about black leaders who "made a business of keeping the troubles, the wrongs, and the hardships of the Negro Race before the public." These men, he claimed in a swipe at his younger, more outspoken rival W. E. B. Du Bois, "do not want the Negro to lose his grievances because they do not want to lose their jobs."[17] Malcolm X later excoriated fellow blacks who sought pity or handouts from whites. That Me, who identified herself as black, would go so hard on African Americans who "act like the world needs to just hand them shit" fit this independence-oriented mindset.

What to make of the allergic reactions toward any mention of race in connection with Tiger's troubles is another matter. Such sentiments might seem to validate the view of those who feel that America still lacks for a more frank collective discussion about racial matters. Every so often, in fact, we hear high-minded calls for what Bill Clinton once termed a "national conversation about race." A recent iteration was Attorney General Eric Holder's controversial speech calling America a "nation of cowards" for our supposed failure to "be honest with one another" and urging greater forthrightness about the problems of prejudice and bigotry. Fedup elaborated in the Tigergate thread on Bossip: "People can say all they want that race has nothing to do with it. Race ALWAYS has something to do with it. Not just with white folks, but blacks as well. We can no longer hide our head in the sand." She shared the premise of Clinton, Holder, and others, mostly on the political Left, that America has never fully reckoned with the injustices of slavery, segregation, and racial violence or the continuing role of race and racism in American life. A version of this belief animates the quest of some black activists and scholars for reparations. The dark legacy of enslavement and oppression, goes the argument, explains why African Americans have not attained equality even today, and healing can occur only through discussion, acknowledgement, and material redress.

But have we really not talked enough about race? Almost forty years ago, Michel Foucault famously challenged the so-called repressive hypothesis, namely the widespread belief that the supposed Victorian legacy of straitlaced prudishness once led us to repress our natural sexual drive and left us out of touch with our bodies.[18] Actually, the great French thinker argued, sex talk was everywhere in the Victorian age and even before, and all the more so with the rise of psychoanalysts, therapists, and an army of other experts in more modern times. Worry about sexuality being repressed, which one still hears today, only helps to guarantee its place as something that we think should be recognized as a core feature of human identity and thus deserving of research, discussion, a required middle-school sex-education class, and trips to the therapist. It's much the same with race. Like sex, we tend to think of race as an "explosive," "charged," "forbidden," or "taboo" topic, a subject not to be brought up at the dinner table and maybe also the workplace. And yet race talk is also ubiquitous. Countless anthropologists, sociologists, historians, political scientists, legal experts, and other scholars teach and write about race relations, a *scientia racialis* to match what Foucault labeled the *scientia sexualis*. The mainstream media may often avoid it, and yet, as was obvious enough from the Tigergate Internet traffic, we do not lack Americans eager to debate the dilemmas of color, heritage, and prejudice, whether in more conventional settings like high-school social-studies classes, college seminars, and workplace diversity training workshops, or in less orthodox ones like Hollywood Gossip, ESPNConversations, and Hip-Hop Wired. The debate is an unruly, cacophonous conversation and sometime shouting match, with its fair share of small-mindedness, name-calling, and snap judgments. And it certainly does not appear headed in the direction that advocates of, say, reparations would wish in the sense of consensus-building about the past's injustices, much less about the best way forward. That national conversation about race is nonetheless already taking place, just not always in the pious, more politically correct tones that one might have expected for so serious a matter.

I think we may talk about race both too much and too little. Everyone has opinions about things racial, and strong ones at that. The exclamation points, bold type, caps, and strong language in the cybercommentary about Tiger's troubles typified the vehement certainty that so often characterizes race talk. Was Tiger a self-hating race traitor? A victim of the white power machine? A "typical" oversexed black man? These and other views were argued with great and sometimes entertaining conviction; yet, for all the ostensible variety of opinion, there was something limited and predictable about the complaints, stereotypes, and arguments and counterarguments, as if we were watching a movie we'd already seen many times before. Whether the black woman aggrieved with Tiger for being with white women or the white man bitter about supposed black privilege, we already knew the lines, or at least most of them. We knew the conclusion in advance too, namely a lack of agreement and the persistence of racial paranoia whether justified or not. By now, even the calls for tolerance and mutual understanding that one hears when race trouble arises—like then candidate Obama's eloquent speech about his controversial ties to a firebrand black minister—seem part of the same familiar drama, as opposed to somehow being above it, as much as one might sympathize with such moderating sensibilities. We are all players, like it or not, in a modern American kabuki theater of race, where our masks too often seem to be frozen into a limited set of expressions.

As an anthropologist, I have my own bit part. At its inception in the post-civil-war years, our discipline spewed dogma about the "lesser races," but to its credit reversed direction in the early twentieth century under the leadership of Franz Boas, the modern American founding father of anthropology. Boas—and his star students, like Ruth Benedict and Margaret Mead—championed the then novel concepts of appreciation for other cultures and the common humanity of people everywhere. The very idea of dividing the species into separate subgroups on the basis of their pigmentation— much less the notion that these "races" somehow varied in ability or intelligence—was a "modern superstition" according to those early anthropologists. Boas, overoptimistically, believed that migration and intermarriage would eventually dissolve any distinctions of phenotype anyway.[19] In the last few decades, anthropologists have more deeply explored the puzzle of just why and how race remains a strong force in society, both in America and abroad. We preach, as Boas did, that the idea of neatly demarcated, biologically inferior or superior "races" is prejudice masquerading as fact, yet also that we must understand the full, sometimes deadly dimensions of race and racism in order to move toward the color-blind society that, in principle, everyone but the diehard racists would like to see someday. I like to imagine, of course, that anthropology offers the more sophisticated, informed talk about race of which we could use more in America. And yet, as I hold forth in lecture, I'm playing a familiar role myself, in this case one akin to the sandal- and love-bead-wearing, wispy-bearded, politically correct teacher Mr. Van Driessen in *Beavis and Butthead*, with his admonitions about peace, love, and the great circle of humanity to his snickering high school class.

One reason that America's race debate has endured has had to do with the unpleasant, eel-like slipperiness of the concept itself. That the color of your skin should matter at all is at once an absurd, preposterous conceit and an unfortunate reality. If you don't talk about persisting structures of racial inequality, they risk not being recognized and thus becoming fixed; if you do discuss them, you run the danger of encouraging finger-pointing, tiresome grievance politics, and the bad social habit of classifying people by race in the first place. Precisely because it has no real basis in scientific fact, the debate about race and racial standing always seems open to some new spin. According to one pundit in the early years, Tiger "injected black macho charisma" to a game once molded on "Jack

Nicklaus's Teutonic discipline," the fist pumps and bold cool taken as evidence for his blackness. By contrast, others had always read Woods as white by virtue of stylistic markers like his, if not nerdy, then suburban Southern California manner of speech and his love for golf. The revelation of Tiger's sexual escapades triggered a whole new back and forth about his racial standing. It's never possible to pin down racial classification because the whole concept's very arbitrariness makes every attempt subjective, conflicting, and unverifiable by its very nature.

We Americans may nonetheless be too self-flagellating about race. If you have traveled to, say, Turkey and heard the things that Kurds, Turks, and Armenians say about one another, America can seem like a bastion of mutual respect and good will. Clearly, too, we are witnessing positive generational changes, among them greater acceptance for interracial romance. But, for now, race remains a nasty quicksand, and, in this sense, it is all the more understandable that Tiger sought to tiptoe around it as much as possible. In early 2008, he was forced to respond to yet more off-key comments, when the Golf Channel anchor Kelly Tilghman joked that younger players should "lynch" Woods in a "back alley" if they hoped to win tournaments. Tiger's "failure" to rush to absolve Fuzzy Zoeller for his "fried chicken and collard greens" comments had drawn ire a decade before, and this time Woods speedily issued a press release calling Tilghman's comments a "non-issue" and saying he knew "unequivocally that there was no ill intent."[20] But this, too, drew criticism, this time from pundits who felt Tiger should have been less forgiving and instead used the incident to educate others about the terrible significance of the word *lynch* for black Americans. His former admirer, the rapper Nas, called Tiger's olive branch to "that white lady" a "coon move," a supposed act of obeisance to the master's will. Blacks and other people of color, especially prominent ones, have what the literary theorist Daphne Patai calls "surplus visibility" about racial matters, always put on the spot when controversy arises.[21] As Tiger discovered once again with the Tilghman gaffe, the problem was that whatever it was that he might say, or not say, was likely to set off new controversy in the polarized racial minefield. Barack Obama followed Tiger's example of trying to keep race mostly off the table for fear of distracting attention from other challenges and somehow inadvertently confirming the secret fears of some white voters that, as a black man, he must somehow be an "obsessed" or "angry" racial partisan. The president's relative silence drew the inevitable criticism, from some civil-rights activists, that he was not doing enough to promote the cause.

Tiger was famous for his ability as a "scrambler," the golf argot for extricating yourself from a sticky situation, like overhanging tree branches blocking your shot or the golf ball being buried in gnarly rough. The great superstar's capacity to escape trouble, the television commentators often remarked, was sometimes magical. His most wondrous scramble, away from golf, may have been to avoid being drawn too far into the swampy water hazard of American race politics and, through the blazing brilliance of his performance, to gain, for the most part, a pass from criticism even from those who felt he was too much the vanilla avoider of race trouble. But, although it may have been the least of his problems amid Tigergate's other humiliations, Woods had been drawn back into the muck, the controversy over his own racial identity opened once again and the ugliest old stereotypes about black men suddenly affixed to him by racist detractors.

Tida Woods had once called her only son the "Cosmic Child." She hoped and expected that Tiger's mixed ancestry and talent would allow him to rise above the petty divisions of heritage and skin.

That had proven a trick that even Tiger could not quite pull off.

7

OUT OF THE WOODS?

The tale of Tigergate had reminded me from early on of Victor Turner's famous concept of the "social drama." The great Scottish anthropologist developed this model from his research in traditional African villages back in the mid-twentieth-century, yet it applies surprisingly well to the peculiar phenomenon of early twenty-first-century celebrity scandal.[1] According to Turner, every society deals with crisis in a culturally ritualized form with four distinct stages: breech, crisis, redressive action, and reintegration. In Tiger's case, the breech was caused by his affairs and their violation of his marriage vows. Crisis followed—the fire-hydrant crash and the rampant bad publicity about his infidelity. Tiger and his people then attempted redressive action, most notably the "apology event," as one cynic termed it. Reintegration was the last stage, though Turner stressed that society does not necessarily accept every transgressor back into the fold. Among other variables, most cultures regard some crimes, like murder, as too serious for there ever to be any widespread reacceptance of those who commit them (and thus, for example, the likes of O. J. Simpson, alleged to have killed his ex-wife and later convicted for armed robbery and kidnapping in another incident, would seem to have little chance of ever regaining much public affection).

Tiger spent most of 2010 dealing with Tigergate fallout. Several of his former mistresses tried to stretch their fifteen minutes of fame. The porn star Joslyn James grabbed gossip-blog attention by cheekily arranging to strip at Milwaukee's Silk Exotic Gentleman's Club in the same week that Tiger was competing nearby, in the PGA Championship. The tabloids also reported that Rachel Uchitel, the New York cocktail hostess, would appear on a new reality show called *Celebrity Rehab*, which followed real-life celebrities, B-list as they might be, as they entered rehab clinics for various addictions. With this, the reality-show phenomenon sank to yet new, Mariana Trench-like depths of trashiness. Tiger and his image managers cannot have been too pleased.

At the year's start, the London bookmakers had given better-than-even odds on Elin divorcing Tiger within six months. It took a little longer than that, but in August the couple announced that their marriage was over. The media marketing of celebrity scandal, as it plays to the chords of sympathy and sentiment, very often follows the wronged woman's travails as part of the drama. There had been various tabloid and gossip-magazine articles with updates from Elin's friends about her emotional state and plans for the future. For a *People* cover story, which Elin said would be her one and only interview, Nordegren said that she "had gone through hell," with her blond hair falling out. She added that she hoped one day to forgive Tiger and wished him well (and also denied the "truly ridiculous" rumor that she had ever beaten her husband over the head with a golf club). Although the sum was not disclosed, some reports fixed her share of the settlement agreement at as much as $750 million. A financial blog speculated that the Swedish krona's sudden rise against the American dollar one late August day may have been caused by the size of the transfer into her bank account. One hoped and guessed that Nordegren, who never wanted the celebrity limelight, would fare well in the end: single, beautiful, and very rich. Elin had a vacation house on a lovely island near her native Stockholm, but decided to keep living in Florida, purchasing a grand old seaside house in Palm Beach with $12 million of her settlement cash. In addition to parenting, she was completing a psychology degree at a local community college. Woods, who was building a new multimillion dollar home of his own just a few miles away, had frequent visitation rights with their children, Samantha and Charlie.

It had been rare to hear any criticism of Tiger whatsoever from inside the golf world before the scandal. His power was such that no one wanted to get on his bad side. He'd been ruthless about expelling from his inner circle those who broke the expected code of silence. When his colorful caddie "Fluff" Cowan apparently took up too much of the spotlight, Woods replaced him with the tightlipped Steve Williams. The burly Williams, who had the charm of a Mafia enforcer, seldom spoke to media. He once threw a fan's $7,000 camera into a pond so the clicking wouldn't bother Tiger.

Tigergate made Tiger vulnerable for the first time. He'd always been something of a hothead on the course, free with obscenities and flinging his clubs after bad shots, all breeches of the hoary gentlemanly etiquette especially expected from top golfers. It's part of the legend of the early-twentieth-century star Bobby Jones that he learned to control his bad temper to become a gracious sportsman. That Tiger, even in his early thirties, still at times behaved like a petulant teenager and had once been excused by reference to his "intensity" and "competitive drive." Now, however, Tom Watson, one of the game's elder statesmen, told a news reporter that Tiger's "swearing and club throwing should end."[2] Even the formerly fawning golf press now made an issue of Tiger's sportsmanship. Lead CBS announcer Jim Nantz criticized Woods for some especially salty tirades on his April return to golf at the Masters.[3] In the spirit of contrition now expected from him, Tiger promptly apologized in a website statement. "I'm trying," he explained, "to do everything I can without losing my fire and competitive spirit."[4] He apparently wasn't making much headway in the following months. One didn't have to be much of a lip reader to tell that his every other word seemed to be "fuck," "son of a bitch," or at least "goddamit," after each of his many bad shots later that year at the British Open tournament, on the hallowed St. Andrews Old Course. "The world No. 1," as a London tabloid noted, "has been slammed for turning the air blue, spitting and hurling his clubs around after wayward shots."[5] A more charitable blogger opined that "cursing is a necessary part of both home carpentry and golf."[6]

Tiger had also lost his mystique. He had once kept us at arm's length, but now we knew all too much about his private life. The original modern golf superstar, Arnold Palmer, had a special charisma, a combination of sex appeal and regular-guy humanity. But, with a few exceptions, American professional golfers nowadays are a colorless lot (for some reason, their international counterparts seem more fun, like the pub-loving Irishman Darren Clarke, the humble South African Louis Oosterhuis, and the ebullient South Korean Y. E. Yang). Now that his aura had been stripped away, Tiger did not seem so different from the other American golfers. He was surely much more than just the celebrity drunk on power, the sex addict, or any of the other one-dimensional caricatures of him in Tigergate's wake. But Woods, now that we knew more at least about his personal life, did not seem an especially compelling personality either (and perhaps this was to be expected of someone who had spent the majority of his waking hours on the planet trying to hit a white ball into a hole).

Tiger had to endure reproachful moralizing from some unlikely quarters. At a press conference on the day before his return to golf at the 2010 Masters, Billy Payne, the chairman of the host Augusta National Club, blasted Woods for having forgotten that "with fame and fortune comes responsibility." "Our hero," as Payne described the disgraced golfer, "disappointed all of us" with his "egregious" off-course behavior and thereby failed "to live up to his expectations as a role model that we sought for our children." He added, "We at Augusta hope and pray that our great champion will begin his new life here tomorrow in a positive, constructive manner," because "his future will never again be measured only by his performance against par, but by the sincerity of his efforts to change."[7]

This was an unlikely case of finger-wagging. Professional golf, where men spend months away from home, has always had more than its share of philandering and broken marriages (a former star, Hal Sutton, was nicknamed "Halimony" for his trail of exes). Never before, however, had the head of the Masters or any other tournament publicly scolded a golfer. It took remarkable hubris and myopia for the Augusta chairman to climb onto the soapbox given his own club's dismal record of discrimination and bigotry. In the old days, the idea of nighttime entertainment for Augusta's wealthy white members was going to a "battle royal," where young black teen-agers beat each other bloody for a few dollars; the club was a proud bastion of Jim Crow that did not admit a black member until 1990. Far from having ever expressed remorse for those policies, club officials tended to take it as an affront when anyone dared to make mention of them. Under the chairmanship of Billy Payne, the club continued to resist calls to end its archaic refusal to admit women. "Who knew," an incredulous newspaper editorialist wrote of the Augusta chairman's scolding of Woods, "that God made a high horse low enough for Billy Payne to saddle?"[8]

Even Tiger's return as a pitchman flopped. Since the first "Hello World" spot, Woods's hip, clever Nike ads had been crucial to building his brand as an inspirational, funny, charismatic, superhuman,

Anonymously doctored photo depicting Tiger with a Nike smile, 2010.

family-loving icon. As the scandal broke, most companies pulled their Tiger ads, but Nike ventured one new spot to mark his return to competition. It was a thirty-second shot of Tiger staring somberly at the camera, with a voiceover from Earl Woods. Although the elder Woods had passed away four years before, the Nike creative people somehow found or engineered audio of him speaking as if addressing his son from beyond the grave in a somewhat reproachful, pseudomystical way: "I want to know what your feelings are. And did you learn anything?" Then the screen faded to black and the trademark Nike swoosh. In the preceding months, critics had drawn parallels between Tiger's caddish conduct and the creepy ubiquity and uneven labor record of the sports-apparel giant for which he was the most famous spokesperson. An anonymous Internet caricaturist had photoshopped Tiger's mouth into the swoosh, or "swoosh-tika," as Nike critics called it, as if to suggest he was both a liar and a tool of the brand. The new Masters ad aimed for edginess and to begin the rehabilitation of its disgraced pitchman by endowing him with a new layer of humanity and humility. But even in a society where just about anything can be commodified, it seemed contrived to turn Tiger's serial philandering and addiction rehab into a television spot. Richard Sandomir, a media critic for the *New York Times*, panned the ad as a lame, distasteful attempt by Woods to "reclaim some sort of moral high ground."[9] The outcome of the 2010 Masters was itself something of a public-relations setback for Tiger. The amiable Phil Mickelson, who had stood by his wife Amy as she fought breast cancer, won the championship. When Phil, Amy, and their two young daughters embraced on the eighteenth green, the announcer Nantz intoned that the Mickelson victory was "one for the family." It was an implicit rebuke of Tiger and his home-wrecking escapades.

Then, too, there was Tiger's golf game. Woods finished a respectable fourth at Augusta, but he was winless for the rest of the year and into 2011. As he himself admitted in several press conferences, his troubles had clearly diminished his famous focus. He split from his swing coach, Hank Haney, and then fired his loyal caddie, Steve Williams (who had dared to break the code of omerta Woods demanded from those closest to him by telling reporters he was "angry" with Tiger for having "let down" his wife and kids). A repeating swing is the underlying key to golf excellence, and Tiger was lacking consistency as he experimented with various new swing changes. Even his putting was now no better than average, a sign of lost confidence. Tiger had established a new benchmark for power, athleticism, and excellence in professional golf, and the competition had also caught up with him. Woods had lost, in particular, his power advantage. Many brawny, supple, and confident twenty-something professionals could now belt the ball past Tiger. The fear factor was gone, too. Even before the scandal, Tiger had been faced down in several tournaments, no longer intimidating his competitors quite as much as in earlier years. The post-Tigergate Woods was just another very good player, and no longer the alpha golfer. Finally, too, Tiger had to deal with injuries, and, in particular, his surgically repaired left knee, which some observers believed might eventually force his early retirement. Tiger's own ultimate golf goal had always been to claim the record for the most career victories in golf's coveted four major championships, namely the Masters, U.S. Open, British Open, and PGA. Holding fourteen titles before Tigergate, Woods was expected to break the mark of eighteen set by Jack Nicklaus, the strong-willed Ohio pharmacist's son who had so dominated the game in his era. That was no longer a sure thing at all.

But all was certainly not lost. Golf's age cycle worked in Tiger's favor, at least if his health held up. Most football and basketball players have retired by their mid-thirties, but Woods was just entering his prime in a sport where many players do not peak until their late thirties or even forties. He had time to regain his old confidence and focused intensity. Although there were many excellent young pros, no single individual had yet emerged as the new dominant golfer. Tiger's earnings declined by almost $20 million in his annus horribilis of 2010, mostly due to lost endorsement money. The richest athlete in history, it turns out, was the ancient Roman charioteer Gaius Applulelius Diocles; he had won the equivalent of $15 billion in prize money on his retirement in 146 A.D.[10] Tiger, with his total net worth being a mere $1 billion or so, would never match that record. Even so, Woods took home $74 million in 2010, out-earning LeBron James, Rafael Nadal, and every other modern sports headliner by a considerable margin. He had 1.7 millon Facebook followers in a further sign of his continuing celebrity no matter for his new vulnerability out on the fairways.

Tiger himself claimed to have emerged a better man for his troubles. "I learned a lot about myself," he told reporters in a videoconference call in late 2010, "and I learned how things went wrong, why they went wrong, and had to take a pretty deep and introspective look at myself. And there wasn't a lot of things I liked about it. But I had to do it, and I did it, and I'm grateful that I did."[11] In a way, Woods had been a prisoner his whole life, in the artificial polo-shirt bubble of golf destiny, first of his father's expectations and then those of his sponsors, fans, and his own harsh standard of excellence. Whether he'd somehow subconsciously wanted to destroy his old self or not, the scandal had certainly freed Tiger from his constraining image as the impeccable straight-arrow champion. He had a chance now to "attain something more human," as the journalist Jaime Diaz put it.[12]

Some signs indicated a man more at ease with himself and the world than he'd been in his ascent to golf glory. Tiger released a chatty iPhone instructional app and started a Twitter account, where he answered questions from fans about his favorite movies and foods. Woods also said all the right things about making his kids his top priority. He even waxed philosophical, the fairway ace as media-studies scholar, about how the scandal has become such a feeding frenzy. "The world has gotten so much smaller," Tiger told a reporter, "If this had happened to someone in the '60s or '70s, it wouldn't have been as big. It wouldn't have gone as global as fast. Our times have changed, and I totally get it."[13]

One wondered, however, about this ostensibly more self-reflective, more accessible Woods. Were we just witnessing more image management? Tiger's insistence that he was now more "blessed and balanced" than ever before, not many months after his marriage had imploded and he'd been made America's laughing-stock, sounded a bit forced and formulaic. The coordinated timing of his post-Tigergate charm offensive—the Twittering, an op-ed in *Newsweek*, an ESPN radio-show appearance—felt like a new advertising campaign, the product roll-out of a chastened, obliging, and thus new and improved Tiger. He was still sometimes curt and condescending at his press conferences. And his agent, Mark Steinberg, spoke frankly about "taking back the narrative" to rebrand Tiger as still "arguably the greatest golfer that's every played," yet also as the star of a feel-good tale about the redemption of a "changed man."[14] Controlling the story meant leaving the scandal's messy details behind. Tiger's people told the ESPN talk-show hosts that the subject of what had actually happened on the night of the crash was off-limits.

That was fair enough. Why should Tiger be obligated to disclose every seamy detail of his personal life? He's already been subjected, after all, to enough ridicule and contempt to become a textbook example of the French anthropologist René Girard's concept of ritual scapegoating.[15] Although the term derives from the ancient Israeli practice of sending a sacrificial goat into the desert in penitence for society's sins, Girard argues that scapegoating occurs in cultures everywhere. In sports, for example, the manager or coach seldom bears the sole blame for a losing season, and yet he's often cut loose in hopes that his firing will lead the athletic gods to smile once again upon the team. According to Girard, the typical sacrificial victim is a child, old person, foreigner, or otherwise vulnerable member of society; in America, however, we also also make scapegoats of our most favored citizens, namely our celebrities. The only real difference between those hapless ancient goats and the modern celebrity is that the Tiger Woodses of our times may be allowed to return from the wilderness into society's good graces if they make the proper ritualized gestures of penitence and humiliation. The media now functions as the kohanim, the ancient Jewish priests; it picks the scapegoats and presides over their expulsion into the desert of lost affection and, of course, endorsement earnings. And so it was that Woods was singled out for supposed crimes—cheating, then lying—that millions of other Americans have committed without suffering the indignity of becoming tabloid headliners. Celebrity scandal is a theater of finger-pointing and the cathartic punishment of transgression in the classic scapegoating tradition.

Thankfully, however, these exercises have a brief shelf-life in an age of short attention spans and instant news. If Tiger had been cru-

cified in this particular passion play, he didn't stay on the cross for
long. He received some scattered heckling in the first months after
his return, including predictable joking about which mistress might
be waiting inside when he went into a Porta-Potty between holes.
But Woods was already on his way to a good measure of Turnerian
reintegration by the 2010 season's end. His late August divorce
announcement drew relatively scant attention; it ranked on that
night's *Inside Edition* beneath a story about Lindsay Lohan's early release from rehab and one about a woman who had locked her cat in
a dumpster. Television announcers, tired of Tigergate, euphemized
Tiger's return to golf as a "comeback" as if he'd had cancer or been
in a car crash.

Fans missed Woods's thrilling old exploits. "I'm hoping for a
Tiger rebound," posted PatMaguire in the Golf.com blog comment
section, "golf on TV sucks cow bells without him."[16] Although some
remained alienated by what they'd learned about his private life,
many people began rooting for Tiger again. His injury troubles and
obvious difficulties in recapturing his golfing magic added a certain sympathy factor into the mix. Even the sanctimonious Billy
Payne came around. In early 2011, he inked a deal involving Tiger,
the PGA tour, and the videogame company EA Sports for the latest
Tiger Woods game to include the iconic Augusta National, with club
profits going to establish a foundation to promote golf worldwide.
Whenever it came, Woods's first post-Tigergate tournament championship was likely to be a big event with cheering crowds and the
full treatment of expectable media clichés about how far he had
come to win again between his divorce, bad knee, and struggles
with his golf game.

I recalled that First Church of Tiger Woods website. It was done
in fun, and yet human beings are always on the lookout for signs of
divinity and the miraculous in a damaged, disorderly world. Tiger
seemed to have touched down from some other realm with his
otherworldly talent, perfect family life, and boundless wealth and

success. Tigergate had broken the spell of that hallucination about Woods's immortal perfection. The disappointed radio-talk-show host-pastor-webmaster of the First Church website had rebaptized it the "The Damnation of Tiger Woods" in good biblical fashion.

But holiness can grow tiresome. You can't have good drama without failure, mistakes, and some surprising plot twists. As banal as they might have been, Tiger's personal troubles had given an unexpected turn to his story, a whole new layer of speculation, doubt, and debate. He'd become a walking reality show as well as a sports superstar. Ever since he toddled onto the set of *The Mike Douglas Show* at the age of two, Tiger had a knack for grabbing attention, albeit not always in ways he might have liked. And he had the better part of a lifetime still ahead of him.

I suspected that Woods would give us much more to ponder and, at least for golf fans, to marvel at in the long years ahead.

Notes

NOTES TO PROLOGUE

1 Woods and McDaniel, *Training a Tiger*.

NOTES TO CHAPTER 1

1 That golf in Scotland is a sport of the people is part of what John Lowerson calls the "homeland myth"; in other words it fixes Scotland as hardy, egalitarian, and rebellious, in opposition to the more snobby and domineering English ("Golf and the Making of Myth." 83). See also Lowerson, *Sport and the English Middle Classes, 1870–1914*. As Lowerson and others point out, golf has also been connected to money, elitism, and exclusivity in Scotland (and, until recently, the game there has been much more closed to women than in the United States). Even so, golf is woven into everyday life in many parts of the country, and Scots of all social classes have enjoyed playing since as early as the seventeenth century. The journalist Lorne Rubenstein's *A Season in Dornoch* is an entertaining account of golf's place in the small northern town of Dornoch, home to the famous Royal Dornoch course.

2 An excellent overview of golf's history in America is George Kirsch's *Golf in America*. Also extremely useful is Richard J. Moss's *Golf and the American Country Club*. Bradley S. Klein, a former political science professor and now

senior writer at *Golfweek* magazine, has published a number of insightful and entertaining books about the game and its development, among them *Rough Meditations*. For some of the most recent scholarship about golf, see a recent special issue of the *Journal of Sports and Social Issues* 34, no. 3 (August 2010).

3 John Strege's *When War Played Through* shows how golf's tradition of charity goes back to the Second World War, including Bing Crosby's and Bob Hope's legendary barnstorming to raise money and spirits among the troops.

4 I played in 1979 on the golf team at Haverford College, which practiced at the Merion Country Club West Course, the lesser-known of its two tracks. One of my teammates, David Chang, discovered that the club did not allow black or Jewish members, and launched a campaign to convince Haverford to cut ties with Merion. This was the end of the Haverford golf team, as it was not able to make arrangements to base itself at another course. The demise of intercollegiate golf at Haverford was not much of a loss as we were not much of a team.

5 Stephen Birmingham's *"Our Crowd"* makes interesting mention of the early world of Jewish country-club golf. See also Moss, *Golf and the American Country Club*.

6 Lazor, "Foreword," 2. *Golf Digest* 19, no. 2 (1968): 27.

7 The quote comes from Don Van Natta Jr.'s entertaining history of golf and the American presidency, *First Off the Tee*, 17.

8 Mackenzie, *The Spirit of St. Andrews*, 261.

9 For a thoughtful exploration of golf's relationship to capitalism and globalization, see Cerón, "An Approach to the History of Golf."

10 Rachel Miyung Joo offers an interesting look at the larger politics of sports and Korean and Korean American identity in "Trans(national) Pastimes and Korean American Subjectivities."

11 A documentary called *The Golf War*, where Tiger Woods makes a cameo, chronicles the negative impact of golf-course development on a Philippine fishing community.

12 Cullen, *Why Golf?*, 47.

13 The case appears in Freud's *Beyond the Pleasure Principle*. Freud, of course, always saw dark forces at work in the human psyche; he suggested that the boy might also be flinging down the wooden spool as an expression of anger, the spool standing in for his mother.

14 Michael Murphy, the author of the cult classic *Golf in the Kingdom*, and Rhea A. White offer a fascinating look at "the zone" in *In the Zone*.

15 Wind, "The Lure of Golf," 404.

16 Latour, *We Have Never Been Modern.*

17 Adatto, "Golf," 467.

NOTES TO CHAPTER 2

1 Nicklaus was repeating what Bobby Jones, the great early-twentieth-century champion, had once said about him.

2 ' In the early twentieth century, before the Masters, the four major championships were considered to be the U.S. and British Amateur and Open Championships.

3 Quoted in Hubert Mizell, "Thirty-four Years of Masters Memories," *St. Petersburg Times,* 4 April 2001. Curt Sampson's *The Masters* is a fascinating history of the tournament. *The Making of the Masters,* by David Owen, is another very interesting read, and attempts to correct some of the more negative caricatures of Roberts and the Augusta National club.

4 The quote comes from an article about Earl Woods and his relationship to Tiger (Smith, "The Chosen One").

5 The webmaster, John Ziegler, was a radio talk show host.

6 Kaufman and Wolff, "Playing and Protesting."

7 Amy Bass's *Not the Triumph but the Struggle* provides a good overview of the Olympics protest. See Grant Farred's excellent *What's My Name?*, on the political life and censure of Muhammad Ali; Farred also points to the less-than-heroic dimensions of Ali's persona, including his denigration of darker-skinned black opponents and his willingness to fight under the auspices of notorious Third World dictators.

8 That Florida has no state income tax is part of its appeal to superstar athletes and others among the super-rich.

9 I draw this information from Weisman, "The Tiger and His Stripes."

10 The fraught subject of race and genetics has provoked much debate. See, for example, Jon Entine's *Taboo: Why Black Athletes Dominate Sports and Why We're Afraid to Talk About It*; a critical "Review of *Taboo*" by the prominent physical anthropologist Jonathan Marks and Entine's subsequent "Letter to the Editor" in response to Marks. John Hoberman argues in *Darwin's Athletes* that the myth of black athletic supremacy has been damaging to black America, among other influences reinforcing the larger and pernicious idea of innate racial differences. His views have also been controversial, and Ben Carrington's *Race, Sports, and Politics* offers one counterpoint.

11 Quoted in Hoberman, *Darwin's Athletes*, 156.

12 It's wise to be skeptical about any claims of a relationship between biology

and sports performance given the ugly history of pseudoscientific racial research. At the same time, with advances in the genomic sciences, a growing body of credible literature does suggest some limited role of genetic variations across human populations in success at particular sports. See for example, Bray et al., "The Human Gene Map for Performance and Health-Related Fitness Phenotypes: The 2006–7 Update." A discussion of fast-twitch and slow-twitch fibers and their relevance for sports can be found in Costill et al., "Skeletal Muscle Enzymes and Fiber Composition in Male and Female Track Athletes." On the concept that allele frequencies of ACTN3, the gene expressed only in fast-twitch muscle fibers, vary from population to population, see Yang et al., "Genotype is Associated with Elite Athletic Performance." And for the idea that genotype may influence and yet by no means determine athletic excellence at the elite level, see Lucia et al., "Citius and Longius (Faster and Longer) with No Alpha Actinin-3 in Skeletal Muscles?" Grateful thanks to Jennifer Wagner for guidance with these citations.

13 As the reader will soon discover, I have not hesitated to quote from Tigergate blog posts and comments in their raunchy, unvarnished detail, including, if you will pardon me, words like "fuck" and "shit." But the epithet "nigger," of course, targets a particular group of people, and I've preferred not to spell it out fully when it appears in posts and comments. Admittedly, as Randall Kennedy's thoughtful *Nigger: The Strange Career of a Troublesome Word* underlines, the term is too deeply rooted to be simply wished away, and the appropriateness or not of its usage depends on the complexities of context. And it borders on censorship, however well-intended, to replace altogether the original word used by an author (or a blog poster) with some more palatable term. This occurred in a controversial recent sanitized edition of *Huckleberry Finn* where the editors substituted "slave" for Twain's own "nigger" and "Indian" for his "injun." I have left in "nigger" when used by Woods internet posters to convey accurately their language and manner of thinking, and yet marking it only as the "n-word" is my imperfect, awkward compromise to avoid having to print the entire ugly term time after time. I've done the same thing with two other favorite epithets of many posters, "bitches" and "hoes," not fully spelling them out either.

14 Quoted in Dolph Hatfield, "The Jack Nicklaus Syndrome—Racism in Sports—The Popular Condition—Column," *Humanist*, 28 February 2011.

15 Steve Sailer, "Are Caublinasians Genetically Superior?," *National Post*, 10 February 2000. I should add that I enjoy much of Sailer's very original writing about golf.

16 Quoted in Jerry Potter, "Tiger's Father Earl Woods Dies at 74," *USA Today*, 3 May 2006.

17 Quoted in Jaime Diaz, "Raising Tiger Hardly Just a Father Affair," ESPN, 8 April 2009, http://sports.espn.go.com/.

18 Tim Marchmann, "Grouped with Tiger? Good Luck . . . ," *Wall Street Journal*, 10 April 2009, w5.

19 Gumbrecht, *In Praise of Athletic Beauty*, 8.

20 The Pelé interview appears in the BBC series *History of Football: The Beautiful Game*, in the "Superstars" episode.

NOTES TO CHAPTER 3

1 Reed Albergotti et al., "How Tiger Protected His Image," *Wall Street Journal*, 18 December 2009. Both Tiger's agent, Mark Steinberg, and the American Media chief executive David Pecker declined to comment about the *Wall Street Journal* story.

2 Callahan, *His Father's Son*.

3 Ibid., 151,

4 Cohen, *Sex Scandal*, 11.

5 Dyer, *Heavenly Bodies*, 210.

6 Ariely, *Predictably Irrational*. Ariely does not mention the pack mentality of journalism specifically, yet it fits very well with his observations about "herding," namely our tendency to make our own decisions about what is good, bad, or important on the basis of those of others, which can create a stampede effect.

7 Gluckman, "Gossip and Scandal."

8 Lewis, *Life in a Mexican Village*. This book was an attack on the previous work on this Mexican village by Robert Redfield, who had portrayed it as a harmonious, collectively oriented place. In a golf-related twist and sign of changing times, the same village, Tepotzlán, just south of Mexico City, became the site of a controversy chronicled by journalist Bruce Selcraig over the construction of a Jack Nicklaus-designed golf course.

9 McLean and Cook, *Headline Hollywood*, 6.

10 Callahan, *His Father's Son*, 200. Callahan reports that Palmer's long marriage to Winnie Palmer was loving nonetheless.

11 Kipnis, *How to Become a Scandal*, 7. John Caughey's *Imaginary Social Worlds* is a useful look at the larger questions of fandom and its pleasures and expectations.

12 Gray, "Anxiety, Desire, and Conflict in the American Racial Imagination."

13 Kevin K. Gaines's *Uplifting the Race* provides an interesting account of early-twentieth-century reasons for black opposition to intermarriage in the case of Johnson and in general.

14 Anthropologist John Hartigan Jr. usefully discusses the Imus case and the racial politics of scandal, in *What Can You Say?*

15 Ward, *Unforgivable Blackness*, 249, 293.

16 Paul Slansky and Arleen Sorkin, eds. New York: Bloomsbury, 2006. Feminist theorist Diane Negra contends that the media often invites us to "root against" female train-wreck celebrities in the vein of Amy Winehouse and Lindsay Lohan, and yet to wish the best for their "troubled male counterparts" such as Heath Ledger, Owen Wilson, and Robert Downey Jr. For her view, see Diane Negra, "The Feminisation of Crisis Celebrity," *Guardian*, 9 July 2008. Negra is right to point out how gender figures into the equation of media sympathy and opprobrium, though one can also think of many exceptions to her argument.

NOTES TO CHAPTER 4

1 Scott, *The Weapons of Weak*. Scott's argument about the "weapons of the weak" has also had its critics, including those who felt he underestimated the power of dominant ideologies to influence the thinking of the subaltern.

2 Darnton, "Presidential Address: An Early Information Society."

3 I should note that Trump is also a luxury golf resort-developer with his own golf-themed reality show on the *Golf Channel*.

4 Diane Nelson in *Reckoning* brilliantly discusses the questions of "duping" and conspiracy theory.

5 Boellstorff, *Coming of Age in Second Life*.

6 Turkle, *Life on the Screen*.

7 Thanks to Nadia Hemady for this insight.

8 I've corrected typos or grammatical infelicities in only a couple of cases, when it seemed necessary to make the post legible.

9 Berlant, *The Female Complaint*, 2.

10 Ibid.

11 Maggie Quale, "Why Do We Care about Lindsay Lohan?" *San Francisco Chronicle*, 30 July 2010, http://articles.sfgate.com/.

12 Fassin and Rechtman, *The Empire of Trauma*.

13 Other self-help groups, all based on the twelve-step method yet different

in their approaches, include Sex and Love Addicts Anonymous, Sexaholics Anonymous, and Sexual Compulsives Anonymous. The Gentle Path program that Tiger apparently attended in Hattiesburg, Mississippi, is not based on the twelve-step method, though Tiger's language in his apology suggested that he was in some sort of twelve-step program, as many of those treated at Hattiesburg also are.

14 Boorstin, *The Image*.

15 Horkheimer and Adorno, *Dialectic of Enlightenment*, 120.

16 Žižek, *The Sublime Object of Ideology*.

NOTES TO CHAPTER 5

1 Barkley and Wilbon, *Who's Afraid of a Large Black Man?*, 236. In the aftermath of Tigergate, Tiger's kindergarten teacher claimed that this story was actually false, AOL News, 2 April 2010, "Kindergarten Teacher Wants to Teach Tiger Lesson in Truth," http://www.aolnews.com/2010/04/02/kindergarten-teacher-wants-to-teach-tiger-lesson-in-truth/.

2 "Racial Stereotyping in Sports Discussed at Academic Conference," press release about a conference on sports and society held at Stanford University while Woods was still a student there, 17 May 1995, available at the website for Stanford University news releases, http://news.stanford.edu/pr/.

3 Ibid.

4 Danzy Senna, "The Mulatto Millennium," 428.

5 "Racial Draft," 24 January 2004, Season Two "The Dave Chappelle Show," *Comedy Central*

6 Woods, "Foreword," 8.

7 Woods appeared on the *Oprah Winfrey Show* on 24 April 1997. I am very grateful to Duke University librarian Linda Daniels for obtaining a transcript.

8 Some critics objected to the ad, asserting that no club barred blacks by 1996.

9 See, for example, an ESPN special about the lack of African Americans in professional golf: Mark Schwarz, "Critic: Woods in Denial about Race," ESPN, 5 April 2009, http://sports.espn.go.com/.

10 Eugene Robinson's *Disintegration* discusses the new class divide within black America.

11 Cohen, *A Consumer's Republic*.

12 In late 2010, the black golfer Joseph Bramlett, also a former Stanford player, earned his one-year tour card.

13 Quoted in Cosgrove, *Social Formation and Social Landscape*, xx.

NOTES TO CHAPTER 6

1 Jackson, *Racial Paranoia*, 7.
2 Wallace, *Constructing the Black Masculine*.
3 Kimmel, *Guyland*, 167.
4 Poulson-Bryant, *Hung*, 7. A classic earlier exploration of these questions of race, sex, and masculinity is Frantz Fanon's classic *Black Skin, White Masks*, originally published in 1952. The great Martinican psychiatrist asserted that whites see black men as a "penis symbol of virility" (136). In reality, Fanon took anatomical relish in insisting that research showed that the fantasy of the oversized black phallus is just that ("the average length of the African's penis, according to Dr. Páles, is seldom greater than 120 millimeters [4.68 inches] . . . the same figure for a European" (147). But, he continued, "nobody is convinced by these facts" (147) and whites preferred to believe in the myth of greater black male sexual potency. Fanon believed that "the Negro" possesses this "hallucinating power" (132) because "the civilized white man retains an irrational nostalgia for the extraordinary times of sexual licentiousness, orgies, unpunished rapes, and unrepressed incest. . . . Projecting these desires onto the black man, the white man behaves as if the black man actually had them" (142). Fanon was never shy about presenting his own sometimes questionable psychoanalytic-cum-anticolonial speculation as if it were unquestionable fact, and yet his writing remains a valuable touchstone for thinking about the strange mirror dance of sexual politics and race relations in modern society.
5 Reilly, *Who's Your Caddy?*, 51.
6 Available at the Huffington Post website, 6 January 2010, http://www.huffingtonpost.com/.
7 Michael Kimmel makes this point in *Guyland*, 169–89.
8 Pierce, "The Man. Amen, ." The article was originally in 1997 published by GQ, but the rights have been purchased by *Esquire*, and it's now most easily available online through http://www.esquire.com/.
9 "Tiger Woods' Text Messages: Sexting Joslyn James," Celebrity Smack, 18 March 2010, http://www.celebritysmackblog.com/.
10 "Text Messages between Tiger Woods and Jaimee Grubbs," *New York Post*, 10 December 2009, http://www.nypost.com/.
11 "Letter to Tiger Woods Elin Divorce, Tiger . .Kobe Bryant,OJ Simpsons and Michael Jackson. . ," Discosean21 channel, YouTube, 27 December 2009, http://www.youtube.com/.

12 D. K. Wilson, "Is Tiger Woods Black Enemy Number One?," 2 December 2009, CounterPunch, http://www.counterpunch.org/.

13 Quoted in John Patterson, "Profile: Spike Lee" in *The Guardian*, The Guide Section, 18 September 18, 2004, 15.

14 See the "NAACP Statement on the Resignation of Shirley Sherrod," July 20, 2010 originally posted on http://www.naacp.org/.

15 It should be noted, in fairness to Tiger, that one of his girlfriends at Stanford was Native American, and always spoke highly of him. She decided to separate from him because she didn't want the role of the golf wife and now works for her tribe. See Irene Folstrom, "Tiger's College Girlfriend Speaks Out," Golf.com, 3 March 2010, http://www.golf.com/.

16 Sam Roberts, "Black Women See Fewer Black Men at the Altar," *New York Times*, 4 June 2010, A12.

17 Washington, *My Larger Education*, 118.

18 Foucault, *The History of Sexuality*.

19 See Baker, *From Savage to Negro Anthropology* and *Anthropology and the Racial Politics of Culture* for much more on Boas and his legacy.

20 Farrell Evans, "Hidden Meaning in Tiger's Reaction to Tilghman's 'Lynch' Remark," Golf.com, http://www.golf.com/.

21 Patai, "Minority Status and the Stigma and 'Surplus Visibility.'"

NOTES TO CHAPTER 7

1 Turner lays out the concept of the "social drama" and its applications in *On the Edge of the Bush*.

2 Jay Busbee, "Tom Watson: Not a Fan of Tiger Woods' Behavior," Yahoo! Sports, 29 January 2010, http://sports.yahoo.com/.

3 Nantz explained he was especially disappointed in light of Tiger's promise to change his ways following the scandal. Shane Bacon, "Jim Nantz Criticizes Tiger Woods Profanity at Augusta," BX 13 April 2010, http://slumz.boxden .com).

4 Tom Weir, "Tiger Woods Apologizes for Language, Thanks Master Fans," *USA Today*, 23 April 2010, http://www.usatoday.com/.

5 "London Tabloids Tame on Tiger Woods," Golf.com, 15 July 2010, http:// www.golf.com/.

6 ButAsForMe, "Tiger Woods Profanity Aired Live on CBS," Free Republic, 10 April 2010, http://www.freerepublic.com/focus/bloggers/.

7 Associated Press, "Payne: Tiger to Be Judged on Sincerity," ESPN, 7 April 2010, http://sports.espn.go.com/.

8   Jason Whitlock, "Augusta National Chairman Lecturing Tiger? Unbelievable Hypocrisy," *Kansas City Star*, 7 April 2010, c1.

9   Richard Sandomir, "Nike Rolls Out Woods Ad with More Questions than Answers," *New York Times*, 7 April 2010, http://www.nytimes.com/.

10 "Back Then," *New York Times*, 14 August 2010, http://www.nytimes.com/.

11 Jim Peltz, "Tiger Hopes to End Year With Victory," *Los Angeles Times*, 18 October 2010, http://articles.latimes.com/.

12 Quoted on the *Charlie Rose Show*, February 19, 2010, http://www.charlierose.com/.

13 Nick Allen, "Tiger Woods Scandal A Year Later: 'I've moved on,'" *The Telegraph*, 24 May, 2011, c2.

14 Tiger left the IMG publicity conglomerate in 2011, and Steinberg came with him.

15 Girard, *The Scapegoat*.

16 Comment posted to "Tiger says knee, ACL not 'doomsday' injury" on 21 May, 2011 at http://blogs.golf.com/.

Bibliography

Adatto, Carl. "Golf." *Motivation in Play, Games and Sports,* ed. Ralph Slovenko and James A. Knight, 458–70. Springfield, Ill.: Charles C. Thomas, 1967.

Ariely, Dan. *Predictably Irrational: The Hidden Forces that Shape Our Decisions.* New York: HarperCollins, 2010.

Baker, Lee. *From Savage to Negro Anthropology and the Construction of Race, 1896–1954.* Berkeley: University of California Press, 1998.

———. *Anthropology and the Racial Politics of Culture.* Durham, N.C.: Duke University Press, 2010.

Barkley, Charles, and Michael Wilbon. *Who's Afraid of a Large Black Man?: Race, Power, Fame, Identity and Why Everyone Should Read My Book.* New York: Penguin, 2005.

Bass, Amy. *Not the Triumph but the Struggle: The 1968 Olympics and the Making of the Black Athlete.* Minneapolis: University of Minnesota Press, 2002.

Berlant, Lauren. *The Female Complaint: The Unfinished Business of Sentimentality in American Culture.* Durham, N.C.: Duke University Press, 2008.

Birmingham, Stephen. *"Our Crowd": The Great Jewish Families of New York.* New York: Harper and Row, 1967.

Boellstorff, Tom. *Coming of Age in Second Life: An Anthropologist Explores the Virtually Human.* Princeton, N.J.: Princeton University Press, 2008.

Boorstin, Daniel J. *The Image: A Guide to Pseudo-Events in America.* New York: HarperColophon, 1961.

Bray, Molly, et al. "The Human Gene Map for Performance and Health-Related Phenotypes: The 2006–7 Update." *Medicine and Science in Sports and Exercise* 41, no. 1 (2009): 34–72.

Callahan, Tom. *His Father's Son: Earl and Tiger Woods.* New York: Gotham, 2010.

Carrington, Ben. *Race, Sports, and Politics: The Sporting Black Diaspora.* London: Sage, 2010.

Caughey, John. *Imaginary Social Worlds: A Cultural Approach.* Lincoln: University of Nebraska Press, 1984.

Cerón, Hugo. "An Approach to the History of Golf: Business, Symbolic Capital and Technologies of the Self." *Journal of Sport and Social Issues* (August 2010): 339–58.

Cohen, Lizabeth. *A Consumer's Republic: The Politics of Mass Consumption in Postwar America.* New York: Vintage, 2003.

Cohen, William A. *Sex Scandal: The Private Parts of Victorian Fiction.* Durham, N.C.: Duke University Press, 1996.

Cosgrove, Denis. *Social Formation and Social Landscape.* Madison: University of Wisconsin Press, 1984.

Costill, David, et al. "Skeletal Muscle Enzymes and Fiber Composition in Male and Female Track Athletes." *Journal of Applied Physiology* 40, no. 2 (1976): 149–54.

Cullen, Bob. *Why Golf?: The Mystery of the Game Revisited.* New York: Simon and Schuster, 2002.

Darnton, Robert. "Presidential Address: An Early Information Society: News and the Media in Eighteenth-Century Paris." *American Historical Review* 105, no. 1 (February 2000): 1–35.

Dyer, Richard. *Heavenly Bodies: Film Stars and Society.* New York: Routledge, 2003.

Entine, Jon. *Taboo: Why Black Athletes Dominate Sports and Why We're Afraid to Talk About It.* New York: Public Affairs, 1999.

———. "Letter to the Editor." *Human Biology* 73, no. 6 (2001): 771–73.

Fanon, Frantz. *Black Skin, White Masks.* Translated by Richard Philcox. New York: Grove, 2008 (1952).

Farred, Grant. *What's My Name?: Black Vernacular Intellectuals.* Minneapolis: University of Minnesota Press, 2003.

Fassin, Didier, and Richard Rechtman. *The Empire of Trauma: An Inquiry into the Condition of Victimhood.* Princeton, N.J.: Princeton University Press, 2009.

Foucault, Michel. *The History of Sexuality: Volume 1: An Introduction.* New York: Vintage, 1990.

Freud, Sigmund. *Beyond the Pleasure Principle*. New York: Norton, 1990.

Gaines, Kevin K. *Uplifting the Race: Black Leadership, Politics and Culture in the Twentieth Century*. Chapel Hill: University of North Carolina Press, 1998.

Girard, René. *The Scapegoat*. Baltimore: Johns Hopkins University Press, 1986.

Gluckman, Max. "Gossip and Scandal." *Current Anthropology* 4, no. 3 (1963): 207–316

Gray, Herman. "Anxiety, Desire, and Conflict in the American Racial Imagination." *Media Scandals: Morality and Desire in the Popular Culture Marketplace*, ed. James Lull and Stephen Hinerman, 35–98. New York: Polity, 1997.

Gumbrecht, Hans Ulrich. *In Praise of Athletic Beauty*. Cambridge, Mass.: Harvard University Press, 2006.

Hartigan, John, Jr. *What Can You Say?: America's National Conversation on Race*. Stanford, Calif.: Stanford University Press, 2010.

Hoberman, John. *Darwin's Athletes: How Sports Has Damaged Black America and Preserved the Myth of Race*. New York: Mariner, 1998.

Horkheimer, Max, and Theodor Adorno. *Dialectic of Enlightenment*. New York: Continuum, 1969.

Jackson, John L., Jr. *Racial Paranoia: The Unintended Consequences of Political Correctness*. New York: Basic, 2008.

Joo, Rachel Miyung. "Trans(national) Pastimes and Korean American Subjectivities: Reading Chan Ho Park." *Journal of Asian American Studies* 3, no. 3 (2000): 301–28.

Kaufman, Peter, and Eli A. Wolff. "Playing and Protesting: Sports as a Vehicle for Social Change." *Journal of Sport and Social Issues* 34, no. 2 (2010): 154–75.

Kennedy, Randall. *Nigger: The Strange Career of a Troublesome Word*. New York: Pantheon, 2002.

Kimmel, Michael. *Guyland: The Perilous World Where Boys Become Men*. New York: HarperCollins, 2008.

Kipnis, Laura. *How to Become a Scandal: Adventures in Bad Behavior*. New York: Macmillan, 2010.

Kirsch, George. *Golf in America*. Champaign: University of Illinois Press, 2008.

Klein, Bradley S. *Rough Meditations: From Tour Caddie to Golf Course Critic, An Insider's Look at the Game*. Hoboken, N.J.: Wiley, 2006.

Latour, Bruno. *We Have Never Been Modern*. Cambridge: Harvard University Press, 1993.

Lewis, Oscar. *Life in a Mexican Village: Tepoztlán Restudied*. Champaign: University of Illinois Press, 1951.

Lowerson, John. "Golf and the Making of Myth." *Scottish Sport and the Making of the Nation*, ed. Grant Jarvie and Graham Walker, 75–90. Leicester, U.K.: Leicester University Press, 1994.

———. *Sport and the English Middle Classes, 1870–1914*. Manchester, U.K.: Manchester University Press, 1995.

Lucia, Alejandro, et al. "Citius and Longius (Faster and Longer) with No Alpha Actinin-3 in Skeletal Muscles?" *British Journal of Sports Medicine* 41, no. 9: 616–17.

Mackenzie, Alister. *The Spirit of St. Andrews*. Chelsea, Mich.: Sleeping Bear, 1995.

Marks, Jonathan. "Review of *Taboo: Why Black Athletes Dominate Sports and Why We're Afraid to Talk About It*." *Human Biology* 72, no. 6 (2000): 1074–78.

McLean, Adrienne, and David Cook, eds. *Headline Hollywood: A Century of Film Scandal*. New Brunswick, N.J.: Rutgers University Press, 2001.

Moss, Richard J. *Golf and the American Country Club*. Champaign: University of Illinois Press, 2008.

Murphy, Michael, and Rhea A. White. *In the Zone: Transcendent Experiences in Sports*. New York: Penguin, 1978.

Nelson, Diane. *Reckoning: The Ends of War in Guatemala*. Durham, N.C.: Duke University Press, 2009.

Owen, David. *The Making of the Masters: Clifford Roberts, Augusta National, and the World's Most Prestigious Tournament*. New York: Simon and Schuster, 2003.

Patai, Daphne. "Minority Status and the Stigma and 'Surplus Visibility.'" *Chronicle of Higher Education*, 30 October 1991, B1.

Poulson-Bryant, Scott. *Hung: A Meditation on the Measure of Black Men in America*. New York: Harlem Moon, 2005.

Reilly, Rick. *Who's Your Caddy?: Looping for Great, Near Great, and Reprobates of Golf*. New York: Broadway, 2003.

Robinson, Eugene. *Disintegration: The Splintering of Black America*. New York: Random House, 2010.

Rubenstein, Lorne. *A Season in Dornoch: Golf and Life in the Scottish Highlands*. New York: Citadel, 2004.

Sampson, Curt. *The Masters: Golf, Money, and Power in Augusta, Georgia*. New York: Villard, 1989.

Scott, James. *The Weapons of Weak: Everyday Forms of Peasant Resistance*. New Haven, Conn.: Yale University Press, 1985.

Senna, Danzy. "The Mulatto Millenium." *Hokum: An Anthology of African American Humor*, ed. Paul Beatty, 429–39. New York: Bloomsbury, 2006.

Smith, Gary. "The Chosen One." *Sports Illustrated*, 23 December 1996, 52–77.

Strege, John. *When War Played Through: Golf During World War 2*. New York: Gotham, 2005.

Turkle, Sherry. *Life on the Screen: Identity in the Age of the Internet*. New York: Simon and Schuster, 1997.

Turner, Victor, and Edith L. B. Turner, eds. *On the Edge of the Bush: Anthropology as Experience*. Tucson: University of Arizona Press, 1985.

Van Natta, Don, Jr. *First Off the Tee: Presidential Golfers, Hackers, Duffers and Cheaters from Taft to Bush*. New York: Public Affairs, 2003.

Wallace, Maurice O. *Constructing the Black Masculine: Identity and Ideality in African American Men's Literature and Culture, 1775–1995*. Durham, N.C.: Duke University Press, 2002.

Ward, Geoffrey C. *Unforgivable Blackness: The Rise and Fall of Jack Johnson*. New York: Knopf, 2004.

Washington, Booker T. *My Larger Education. Being Chapters from My Experience*. Garden City: Doubleday, 1911.

Weisman, Jan. "The Tiger and His Stripes: Thai and American Reactions to Tiger Woods's (Multi-) 'Racial Self.'" *The Sum of Our Parts: Mixed Heritage Asian Americans*, ed. Teresa Williams León and Cynthia L. Nakashima, 231–44. Philadelphia: Temple University Press, 2001.

Wind, Herbert Warren. "The Lure of Golf." *Sport and Society: An Anthology*, ed. John T. Talamini and Charles H. Page, 397–412. Boston: Little, Brown and Company, 1973.

Woods, Earl, and Pete McDaniel. *Training a Tiger: A Father's Guide to Raising a Winner in Both Golf and Life*. New York: HarperCollins, 1997.

Woods, Tiger. "Foreword." *Uneven Lies: The Story of African-Americans in Golf*, by Pete McDaniel, 8–9 Greenwich: American Golfer, 2000.

Yang, Nan, et al. "Genotype is Associated with Elite Athletic Performance." *American Journal of Human Genetics* 73: 627–31.

Žižek, Slavoj. *The Sublime Object of Ideology*. New York: Verso, 1989.

Acknowledgments

Special thanks, for their help and encouragement, go to Doug Campt, Tina Campt, Hugo Cerón, Matt Cohen, Bradley Klein, Grant Farred, Linda Daniels, Eric Smith, Lewis Taylor, Sara Seten Berghausen, David Jamieson-Drake, Edward Gomes, Peter Lange, Matt Cohen, William O'Barr, Diane Nelson, Edward Wanambwa, Jennifer Wagner, Ralph Litzinger, Angela O'Rand, Heather Williams, Bruce Selcraig, Lee Baker, Ebrahim Moosa, Walter Mignolo, Tony Perez, Mark Anthony Neal, Serkan Yolacan, Ed Ibarguen, Reeve Huston, Arturo Escobar, Marisol de la Cadena, Randy Matory, Paul Chaat-Smith, Steve Rubenstein, and Kregg Hetherington. Catherine Lutz and Jaime Diaz, both extraordinarily generous people and terrific writers, commented on the whole manuscript. Jaime helped me obtain permission to reprint several photographs from *Golf Digest* with kind help from Christian Ioos at the magazine. Ken Wissoker has been a treasured friend and editor for almost two decades now. Additional thanks to Leigh Barnwell, Katie Courtland, and Neal McTighe at the press. My beloved friends Anne Allison and Charles Piot have always been there for me. Frances and Randolph Starn are wonderful critics, not to mention fabulous parents and grandparents; I owe them so much more than I can say. My children, Ray and Frances, give me great pride and joy. Katya Wesolowski had faith through hard times, and her intelligence, encouragement, and love makes everything possible.

Index

Accenture: airport billboards and, 26; role of, in Enron scandal, 43

Adatto, Carl, 22

Adorno, Teodor, 65

African Americans, xv, 4–5; debate about Tiger Woods being "black enough," 93–94; discrimination in golf against, 2–4; Greensboro Six and, 74–76; interracial marriage and, 49, 97–99; the Langston Golf Club and, 5; myth of black athletic superiority, 27–28; stereotypes about black masculinity and, 89–91; Tiger Woods as a "racist" and, 96; Tiger Woods as victim of white racism and, 93. *See also* Race

Aldrin, Buzz, 10

Anthropology, xii–xiii; Internet research and, 56–57; race and, 102–3; of sports, xiv

Apology, 17; the "apology event" and, 108; celebrity scandal and, 49–51; by Tiger Woods, 54, 60, 62, 65

Arantes do Nascimento, Edson ("Pelé"), 34

Ariely, Dan: concept of "herding" and, 43

Asian Americans: in professional golf, 79

Athletes: social activism and, 25

Augusta National Golf Club, 4, 23. *See also* Masters Championship

Banks, Eural, 5

Barkley, Charles, 24, 67, 71

Begay, Notah, 32

Berlant, Lauren: concept of "female complaint" and, 60–61

Black. *See* African Americans

Boas, Franz, 102–3

Geertz, Clifford, xiv
Gingrich, Newt, 96
Girard, René: concept of ritual scapegoating and, 116
Gluckman, Max, 44
Golf: African Americans and, 5; the
American dream and, x, 9; capitalism and, 8; "Caucasians-only"
clause of, 4, 76; civil rights movement and, xv, 74–76; the Cold War
and, 10–11; conservatism of professional golfers and, 79; discrimination in, 2–4; dislike for, 1–2;
environmental issues and, 19–20;
frustration of golfers with, 13–14,
21–22; global growth of, 11–12; the
"golf gene" theory and, 14; honesty
and, 46; Jewish country clubs and,
5; lack of diversity in professional
golf, 77–79; luck and, 18–19; mental aspect of, 29–30; moon landing
and, 10; as pastime of businessmen
and politicians, xv; role of, in American society, xiv–xv; the "R.V. syndrome" and, 21; the U.S. presidency
and, 9; "wondrous flexibility" of, 21;
World Anti-Golf Movement and, 2
Golf equipment, 17–18
Gray, Herman, 48–49
Green, Hubert, 30
Greensboro Six, 74–76
Gregory, Ann, 75
Grubbs, Jaimee, 92
Guevara, Ernesto (Che), 11

Hagen, Walter, 78
Haney, Hank, 113
Hogan, Ben, 13

Holder, Eric, 100
Horkheimer, Max, 65
Hurston, Zora Neale, xiii

Imus, Don, 49
International Management Group
(IMG), 34
Internet: anonymity and, 58, 62, 86;
anthropology research and, 56–57;
concept of "second self" and, 57; as
"culture of sadism," 62; racial jokes
and, 86
Ishikawa, Ryo, 2

Jackson, John L., 86
James, Joslyn, 39, 90, 108
Jay-Z (Shawn Corey Carter), 8
Jefferson, Thomas, 45
Jim Crow. See Race
Johnson, Dustin, 29
Johnson, John Arthur (Jack), 48–49
Jones, Robert Tyre, Jr. (Bobby), 109;
code of gentlemanly honor and,
46
Jones, Marion, xvii
Jordan, Michael, 28, 71, 90; avoidance
by, of controversy, 25; competitive
drive and, 32

Kaufman, Peter, 25
Kennedy, John F., 9
Kopnis, Laura, 47
Knight, Phil, 23

Langston Golf Club, 5
Latinos: role of, in golf course main-
tenance, 81–83. See also Rodriguez,
Juan (Chi Chi); Trevino, Lee

Woods, Earl (*continued*)
    93, 112; training by, of Tiger, xviii,
    30–31, 78
Woods, Elin. *See* Nordegren, Elin
Woods, Kultida (née Punsawad)
    (Tida), 27–28, 31–32, 38, 41, 60,
    72, 93
Woods, Tiger: apology of, 52–53;
    "blackening" of, 94; black women
    and, 97; as Cablinasian, 68–71, 73,
    91, 93, 97; childhood of, xviii; the
    First Church of Tiger Woods, 24,
    117; influence of, on professional
    golf, 26; injury troubles of, 114;
    intimidation by, 33; jokes about,
    42; jokes told by, 91; "lighten-
    ing" of, 96; on *Mike Douglas Show*,
    ix–xi, 118; myth of black athletic
    superiority and, 27–28; Nike and,
    23; obsession with penis size and,
    xvii, 89–91; parallels of, to Barack
Obama, 36–37, 70–73; passion
and, 58–59; popularity in Asia and,
26–27; "Racial Draft" skit and, 69;
racial identity and, 67–68, 91–92;
rise to fame of, 23–24; sex addiction and, 52, 62–63; "sexts" sent
by, 40, 92; stereotypes about black
masculinity and, 89–91; Tiger
Woods Foundation as, 25; use of
bad language by, 109–10; videogames, xi; wedding of, 49–50
World Anti-Golf Movement, 2
Wright, Ben, 49

Zaharias, Babe Didrikson, 2
Zedong, Mao, 13; China as "golf-free"
    zone and, 11
Žižek, Slavoj, 66
Zoeller, Fuzzy: incident at Masters
    and, 71, 104

ORIN STARN is a professor of Cultural Anthropology and History and Chair of the Cultural Anthropology Department at Duke University. He is the author of *Ishi's Brain: In Search of America's Last Wild Indian* and *Nightwatch: The Politics of Protest in the Andes*. He is co-editor of *The Peru Reader: History, Culture, Politics*; *Indigenous Experience Today*; and *Between Resistance and Revolution: Cultural Politics and Social Protest*.

Library of Congress Cataloging-in-Publication Data
Starn, Orin.
The passion of Tiger Woods : an anthropologist reports
on golf, race, and celebrity scandal / Orin Starn.
p. cm.
Includes bibliographical references and index.
ISBN 978-0-8223-5199-3 (cloth : alk. paper)
ISBN 978-0-8223-5210-5 (pbk. : alk. paper)
1. Woods, Tiger. 2. Golfers—United States—Biography.
3. Sex scandals—United States. I. Title.
GV964.W66S74 2012
796.352092—dc23
[B]
2011027557